I BELIEVE
IN THE CHURCH

I BELIEVE
IN THE CHURCH

Elmer G. Homrighausen

ABINGDON PRESS

New York • *Nashville*

I BELIEVE IN THE CHURCH

Copyright © MCMLIX by Abingdon Press

All rights in this book are reserved.
No part of the book may be reproduced in any manner
whatsoever without written permission of the publishers
except brief quotations embodied in critical articles
or reviews. For information address Abingdon Press,
Nashville 2, Tennessee.

Library of Congress Catalog Card Number: 59-7247

SET UP, PRINTED, AND BOUND BY THE
PARTHENON PRESS, AT NASHVILLE,
TENNESSEE, UNITED STATES OF AMERICA

TO THE CHILDREN

Richard James
Ruth Karolyn
Elmer Paul
David Karl
Mary Elizabeth
John Frederick

Born into the Christian community; steeped in the heritage, spirit, and reality of the Church; nurtured by the many agencies and influences of the Church; and guided, we pray, into a mature membership in that community, a growing commitment to Jesus Christ, and a creative life of service to God and man in the common life in obedience to the Lord of history

CONTENTS

CHAPTER ONE

THE CHOSEN COMMUNITY

THE CHURCH IS THE CHOSEN COMMUNITY!

How did the Church come to be? How old is it? Visitors to the "eternal city" of Rome are shown churches that were built on a pagan circus, or on the spot where tradition says Paul was martyred, or the place where Peter was crucified. The Mar Thoma Church of South India claims to have been founded by the apostle Thomas in the first century; the Coptic Church of Egypt dates its history from its founding by the evangelist Mark. These churches are old. Yet, there was a time when Christian churches did not exist. But the reality behind them, the eternal Church, originates in the will of God.

God wills the Church

We trace the Church back to God's nature and to his purpose for us and for our world. There is a divine purpose for man and history. Christ Jesus revealed this purpose, and the Church embodies and witnesses to it. It is God's will to sum up all things in Christ, to bring all things under his rule.

As we look about us, we see that all things are not yet under God's rule. When God created all things, he made them good. But something terrible has happened to God's good intention. In place of unity, harmony, and peace, the world is full of disunity, disharmony, and strife. Something went wrong. Man, through his willful disobedience to God and his self-centered living, has fouled up God's good intention. But God has not abandoned the world. While he lets man "stew in his own juice" by letting him suffer the consequences of his sinful ways, God seeks to salvage the situation. He intervenes to restore the lost harmony and re-establish unity. God is love, and because he is love, he wills and works to bring all things under his sway. He wills the Church, the chosen community. He wills that the whole world become a community.

The people who wrote the New Testament never thought of the Church as merely a group of people who were interested in religion or in living the "good life." To these writers the Church was created by God. God took the initiative. The Church resulted from his merciful action. They called it the "church of the living God, the pillar and ground of the truth." So, people do not join the Church just to build a church. They join it because they have been called to belong to the person, the cause, and the community of Jesus Christ.

Paul refers to the Church a great many times in his writings. Only he did not always use the word "church." He thought of the Church as the result of God's work to redeem men through his son, Jesus Christ. It is not an organization thought up by men. Rather it is a community of people who are called by God and who have responded in faith to Jesus Christ. Nothing else could have brought the Christian Church into being.

The Old Testament is the story of God's "chosen" people. God spoke to men in Old Testament days. Later, he spoke to them through his Son. And he further implemented his purpose, and continued Christ's ministry through the Holy Spirit at and since Pentecost. The

Church is God's chosen servant. It is the instrument he has chosen to use in doing his redeeming work in the world.

Was there no church before Jesus' birth? Indeed there was! God created the people of Israel. He called Abraham to be the "father" of a faithful people. All through the Old Testament God's purpose for the world is emphasized as he sought to reveal himself to all men through Israel—his chosen people. But all of the people of Israel did not always fulfill God's purpose for them. Prophets pleaded with them to repent and in faith to return in obedience to God. The prophets proclaimed the hope of a "faithful remnant." While the people of Israel as a whole failed God, there were a few who kept his purpose alive. They were the "faithful remnant," the true Israel. God's purpose did not fail in spite of the disobedience of men.

Jesus did not repudiate Israel. He did not come to destroy the Old Testament church. He came to fulfill it; that is, to fill it to the full of its true meaning. He regarded himself as the Messiah of God's people, the chosen Servant of Jehovah, the Suffering Servant, the Son of Man. As a true son of Israel he sought to make the people of Israel see and accept their true nature and mission. But most of them refused. As a result, the early Christians, the Israelites, broke with the Old Testament community. They took the gospel everywhere. They transplanted the purpose of God into the soil of humanity. They regarded themselves as the true, the fulfilled Israel. They were the founders of God's new community open to all men. And wherever men believed in Jesus Christ, the Church came into being.

God wills the Church! He is not interested in saving individuals by themselves. He seeks to create for himself a people—a fellowship of faith, hope, and love. Love is his very nature. His love is an aggressive power. It is a

11

socializing force. It is a power that reaches out for men and brings them together. It is a power that redeems. It is the ultimate reality in the universe. God wants his people to live in harmony, unity, and fellowship with him and with one another. Like the father in the parable of the prodigal son, God seeks fellowship with his children. He takes the initiative in bringing them home. We can see his love best in the life and suffering and death of Jesus Christ. Jesus' broken body and shed blood are at the center of the life of the Church. They witness to God's self-giving love acting to bring people to himself and to fellowship with one another, even when that love is despised and rejected.

By its nature the Church is a part of the gospel—the Good News. It is not an extra, tacked on to the gospel. We could not have Christianity without a church! Individual Christianity is an impossible contradiction. The Church is the redeemed and redeeming community. It is the fellowship of the forgiven and the forgiving. We may say that the Church is necessary and integral to God, to the Christian, and to the world.

Christ loved the Church

"Husbands, love your wives, even as Christ also loved the church, and gave himself for it; . . . that he might present it to himself a glorious church, not having spot, or wrinkle, or any such thing; but that it should be holy and without blemish." This is what Paul says about Christ's relation to the Church. Christ wished to make it pure and perfect and glorious. Paul goes on to speak of the love and respect that a good husband shows toward his wife, and he likens this to the relation between Christ and the Church. As a husband and wife are one, so Christ and the Church are one. They cannot be separated. Of course, this is a "mystery." Wherever Christ is, there is the Church; wherever the Church is, there is Christ.

All through the Bible, God's desire for fellowship with his children is expressed, even though they sometimes forget him and rebel against him. This spirit is perfectly expressed in Jesus' life, teaching, ministry, and death. His fellowship with his Father was most intimate and unique. He always sought to bring other people into the same kind of fellowship.

Jesus based many of his parables on the theme of fellowship. The prodigal son lost his fellowship with his father because of his rebellious interest in himself. To be saved he had to return to his father's home and love and to a new relationship with his father. The sheep was lost because of its self-centered appetite. It was saved only as it was brought back to the shepherd and to the flock. The lost coin fell from the string of coins that women in those days wore on their foreheads. It was saved only when its owner found it and restored it to its place with the other coins.

The teachings of Jesus are social in implication. No one can read the Beatitudes and fail to see that they are meant for a company of people. The Lord's Prayer is corporate in nature. Jesus often taught one person, but he always sought to show the relationship of this person to himself and to other people. We think of the miracles as signs Jesus performed in public, not in private. They were signs witnessing to God's power among men. The truth that Jesus spoke was "churchly," or social, truth.

Jesus regarded himself as the Messiah, the one sent from God. He was engaged in a corporate mission, for all Israel and the whole world. The word "messiah" is never used in the Bible to refer to an individual savior of individuals. It is always used in connection with a group. The messiah is the anointed leader of a holy community. Nor did Jesus work alone. He called twelve men, his disciples, to be with him. They were the twelve "pillars" of the true Israel. He spoke of himself as the bridegroom of a wedding party, and he regarded his coming as a wedding festival. He is the Good Shepherd. To think of a shepherd, is to think of a flock. He spoke of himself as a vine with its branches, which get their nourishment, indeed their very life, from the vine.

Jesus' death was a public event. It took place in the midst of the world, at the hands of the world, and it had vast significance for the world. It has had widespread consequences in history and among men. He died because of man's sin and for man's salvation. He was the Suffering Servant, dying for his people. During his last supper with his disciples he spoke of the bread as his body and of the wine as his blood that was shed for them. The Church is the community of the broken body and the shed blood. It is the resurrection community that shares in Christ's victory and in his risen power.

In the New Testament letters, Christ and the Church are never separated. Whoever comes to Christ comes to the Church; whoever comes to the Church comes to Christ. The Church is the embodied revelation of our living Lord. It is the body of Christ. There is a living unity between Christ and the Church, and through Christ there is a unity among all members of the Church.

Once we see that Jesus loved the Church and gave himself that it might come into real being, we can better understand the whole Bible—the New Testament in particu-

14

lar. The Bible is a "community" book from beginning to end.

The Holy Spirit creates the Church

God wills the Church, and Christ loves the Church. But a power is needed to make this will and this love work among men, or there could be no church. The Church is created by the power of the Holy Spirit.

This was the meaning of Pentecost. The disciples believed in God; they had lived with Jesus. But the real meaning of Jesus' words, works, death, and resurrection had not come home to them. They had not had an inner experience of Jesus' power. On the day of Pentecost they were gathered together in the upper room. They engaged in prayer, fellowship, discussion, and deep thought. Then something happened! A sound like the rush of a mighty wind filled the room, and tongues of fire appeared. The disciples became filled with the Holy Spirit and began to speak about Jesus with a new power of witness. Jesus was no longer merely a figure of the past. He now became a living power within—within each of them, and within the little Christian community. God in Christ now became a dynamic experience!

To be sure, the Holy Spirit has always been at work in the world and within men. The prophets spoke the word of God through the power of the Holy Spirit. We might say that all high thoughts and worthy ideals and noble purposes have been inspired in some way by the Spirit. The Spirit is at work in all of creation—and always has been. He is the "executive" of the Trinity. What happened at Pentecost was that through Christ Jesus the Spirit now worked in the Church in a special way. The Church became the place where the saving power of Christ became concentrated among men. If we would find the power of God to change people and to change history, we must find it in the Church.

Pentecost was an astonishing event! When we think of those simple people giving a fearless and ardent witness to an inner experience of God, we are amazed. Pentecost marks the birth of a new community—a new order among men. What the disciples became was not due to their own merits. It was due to a Power outside of them that took hold of them and gave them new life. In a way, they began to become what Christ was and had come to share. What Jesus "began to do and teach" was now continued in a new way. Jesus promised to send his disciples a "substitute" in his place—the Holy Spirit. At Pentecost this promise was fulfilled. Jesus became present in a new way.

Through the power of the Spirit, Christ came alive in the hearts and minds and wills of his people. Christians now received the gifts of the Holy Spirit—the very qualities of Christ himself. Through the Spirit they were given the power to pray, to love one another, to understand the things of Christ, and to witness for him. They became a meaningful, missionary, and hopeful company. The Spirit helped them to make right choices. The Spirit created the Church; the Spirit gave the Church understanding and power. Love, joy, peace, patience, kindness, goodness, faithfulness, meekness, and temperance—these are the fruits of the Spirit.

Of course, the reality of the Spirit is dangerous. It has filled some Christian people with such inner enthusiasm and "power" that they have become fanatics on many subjects. Time and again formal churches have had to criticize fanatical sects. Some of these sects have gone beyond the bounds of Christian grace and decency in expressing what

16

they call the "religion of the Spirit." The Bible says we are not to believe every spirit, but we are to "try the spirits whether they are of God, because many false prophets are gone out into the world." We must test the spirits by the measure of love that is in Christ. Love "doth not behave itself unseemly." But no church dare quench the Spirit!

Today we greatly need to renew the life of our churches. Many people believe in God and in Jesus. But they have not had an inner experience of the Holy Spirit. They lack the enthusiasm, the inspiration, and the power the apostles had. When a church is no longer filled with the power of the Holy Spirit, it is no longer Christ's Church. It may have the outward form but it lacks the inner quality of Pentecost.

The Church is necessary

No religion can live in this world without organization. In fact, nothing can live without some kind of form and order. Education has its schools, teachers, libraries, and class schedules, which make it into an organized process. The same is true of music and medicine and law. Christianity, too, must have an organization if it is to live and to be effective in the world. And it must be organized around weak and sinful people; there are no other kind! "We have this treasure in earthen vessels." Every Christian ideal must be expressed through man as he is, and he is never perfect. A Christianity that is not organized will soon be lost in complete chaos. The glory of our Christian faith is that it is expressed through man, imperfect and sinful though he is, and that it is expressed in organized form. God in his mercy chooses to dwell among his people as they are. This is part of the Gospel message: God gives lonely and sinful

people a fellowship-home; he is not ashamed to dwell with them.

In fact, all the faults we find in the Church today were also in the early Church. The letters in the New Testament reveal such faults of the men who make it up. The Church is the world, but it is the world in which God's redeeming power is at work.

While Christianity is not possible without organization, we must always be alert lest its organization smother its life. The two must go together, yet they will always be in tension. Life without organization is chaos; organization without life is tyranny. Because the Church is a living fellowship of persons, its organized life is of supreme importance. The way in which a church is organized should be true to its nature and function as a community of Christ's people. Church organization and administration are very important.

The person needs the Church

William James and Alfred N. Whitehead made practically the same remark about religion. They both called it a personal matter. James defined it as the feelings, acts, and experiences of individual men in their solitude as far as they understand themselves to stand in relation to whatever they think of as the Divine. Whitehead defined religion as a man's experience of the Divine in solitude. As far as they go, these ideas are correct. Being a Christian is a lonely matter. No one else can become religious for us. Nor can we have what Christianity has to offer unless we commit ourselves personally to God. It is the Church's major task to insist on personal Christianity.

But Christianity is not a purely personal matter. No one becomes a Christian by himself. He receives the gos-

pel from Christians of past centuries. The Church has preserved Christianity. It brought the books of the Bible together under the inspiration of the Holy Spirit. It kept alive the heritage of our faith—in biography, art, literature, prayer and devotion, creeds, and in ways of worship. If a man would know Christianity, he must learn it from the Church. Though a man may read the Bible for himself, he must remember its books would not have been canonized, preserved, or translated except for the fellowship of the Church. And unless he goes to church, he may interpret the Bible rather badly by himself.

Furthermore, the Christian man has a psychological need to seek out his fellow Christians for worship, counsel, fellowship, and common service. If he would keep alive a spirit of reverence and if he would grow in grace and knowledge, he needs to worship and to learn in the house of God. He needs the correcting and challenging discipline of the Christian group. Church fellowship still has the power to keep the Christian from doing wrong. It also has a prodding effect upon people who are spiritually dull. Its high demands on the Christian's life produce much self-sacrifice. In the battle against evil the Church is an "armory" for those who are putting up a loyal fight for righteousness.

Where two or three Christians are gathered together, there in their midst is the presence of Another. When they gather together in a fellowship of truth, love, faith, and hope, they experience a group spirit that kindles the loyalty and devotion of each of them. The Church is the center of holy memories, the house of continuous prayer, the treasury of the great tradition, the community where we find it easy to catch the meaning and power of the Christian faith. Through the spirit, worship, prayer, music, fellowship, and creeds of the Church, each of us knows Christianity from the inside.

Even though each prophet of the Old Testament had his own fiercely individual ideas, he never thought of himself apart from the Old Testament community. These prophets were enemies of formal religion; yet they did not think of religion in a purely individual way. If we interpret Christianity only in individual or church terms, we do not do it justice. For Christianity is both.

Christianity is community

In both the Old and New Testaments the Church is made so real that some theologians maintain that God did not reveal himself merely to one man but to a community of people—people whose lives centered in him. The nature of revelation is community inducing and producing. Thus the gospel was a social gospel from the very beginning.

The distinctive thing about the Church is that it is God's creation. It is his beloved community in the earth. It is his means of calling men into fellowship with himself and with each other in grace and truth. The center of the Church is Jesus Christ. In the Church, God in Christ dwells with people in the Spirit, and through it, people find comradeship in a common witness and service to the gospel.

CHAPTER TWO

THE BODY OF CHRIST

THE CHURCH IS THE BODY OF CHRIST!

One of the highest conceptions of the Church is that it is the body of Christ. Paul used this expression in his letter to the Ephesians. He spoke of "the church, which is his body." Of all descriptions of the Church in the New Testament this one is dearest to Christian people. It describes best the Church's real nature. Yet theologians have debated over the term a great deal. These debates have resulted in opposing ideas on the body of Christ.

The holy catholic church

It is difficult to make clear the reasons why there have been such sharp differences over the nature of the Church. There are high-churchmen, who have an exalted idea of the Church. To them, it is a divine institution which God established and which he continues to preserve and extend. It is administered by clergy who hold divine orders. People come to such a church to receive the benefits of salvation, but they are not integral members of it. In an ecumenical gathering, we once heard a high-churchmen protest against criticisms which were made of the Church. He said the Church could not sin! It was holy and perfect and in a class by itself. Now, to be sure, there is a holy side to the Church; it was founded by God and not by men. It is divine! And yet it is human! To say that the

21

Church is only holy is to deny its human reality. As the body of Christ, it must be both holy and human.

There are low-churchmen who would use the term "body of Christ" with caution. They, however, are eager to claim that as the Son of God took on human flesh, so the Church takes on human form. To such churchmen, the Church is composed of people who are gathered to Christ by personal response. They fear a church which has become so holy that it loses its identification with humanity, assumes a proud attitude of perfection, and acts in a dictatorial and authoritarian way for God.

There is a paradoxical relation between the Church, visible and invisible, divine and human, triumphant and militant, heavenly and earthly. The two are organically associated and must never be separated; they must exist in continuous and creative tension.

Perhaps, the proper interpretation of this dilemma is to hold that the Church is both holy and human, visible and invisible, united and divided. The Church is both the *Una Sancta,* the one holy catholic Church; and that Church is in all churches which profess Jesus Christ as Lord and Saviour. The Church seeks to make the churches into *the* Church. However, the term "body of Christ" is only *one* term found in the New Testament to describe the high nature of the church which in mercy lives within these low churches which we know. This is the essence of the Incarnation of the Son of God in human flesh.

Emerson regarded an institution as the lengthened shadow of one man. Movements and organizations often grow out of the work of one man. He is a person so interested in a cause that he becomes the cause itself. He inspires others to put what he saw and achieved into an organization dedicated to carry out his vision. We find it difficult to think of our country without thinking of George Washington and Abraham Lincoln. We associate electricity with Edison, radio with Marconi, music with Bach, philosophy with Plato, and nursing with Florence Nightingale.

In this way we think of the Church as the body of Christ. To be sure, there is a real difference between Jesus and other men. There is a real difference between the Church and a nation, a factory, or an institution. And there is a real difference between religion (God) and all other interests of life. The Church is the work of Jesus Christ. It is the visible sign and instrument of everything he seeks to do for men, in men, and through men. The Church is his creation alone, made to carry on his work until the end of time. It is more than the *shadow* of a man. It expresses in a continuing community all that Jesus Christ said and was and did. It brings to fuller development and expression what he could only begin in Palestine. And it is his body. What he started back in Palestine has grown into a universal community. The Church is as unique as Jesus Christ is unique.

The Church is a living reality

As the body of Christ, the Church is a living thing. Emil Brunner says that the Church uses an organization, but it is an *organism*. It is people and not buildings and organizations. It is a fellowship of believing and loving people.

In the play *A Servant in the House,* by Charles Rann Kennedy, Manson tells the bishop that the Church "is a living thing." It is not a "dead pile of stones and unmeaning timber." "As you enter the Church, and if you listen long enough," says Manson, you "will learn that it is made up of the beating of human hearts, of the nameless music of men's souls." But he cautions, you must see the Church through certain eyes. If you would hear the music of the Church and sense the heartbeats that throb in the body of Christ, you must have ears that are in tune to the things of the Spirit.

The Church, like the human body, is wonderfully and fearfully made. The body has a skeleton to give it form and strength. But even its bones are alive; they live and grow. The body is a mass of tiny cells all with lives of their own. It is made up of many parts all working together. Each different part serves the whole body. So it is with the Church, the body of Christ.

The Church is the agent of Christ

The Church is the agent of the head that controls it. This head is Jesus Christ. He is the directing mind and living power that creates the Church and gives it a purpose.

Someone has said that since the Church is the body of Christ, it should do everything that Christ would do if he were here in person today. But the Church is an "earthen vessel." It is made up of men who are not perfect. No one would think of identifying absolutely our local churches with Jesus Christ. Yet, the amazing thing is that Christ does use "earthen vessels" to continue his work on earth. The miracle of the gospel is that the Son of God does identify himself with finite and sinful humanity. Christ lives on in the fellowship of the finite and sinful people who believe in him. There is no perfect church on earth. And there is no other kind of church which will continue to do Christ's work in the world.

24

When a church takes part in Christ's divine nature, through faith, it becomes united in his truth and grace. It partakes of his nature and mission. The Church is the mission! It preaches the gospel. It draws people into its membership. It worships God through Christ. It unites people who are isolated and estranged from one another. It ministers to people in need with the kind of compassion that was in Christ. Believers find a warm and stimulating comradeship within it. The Church is the place in this world where Christ lives with men and works through them. Though they cannot see him, his presence is real in them through the power of the Holy Spirit. It is in the fellowship of the Church that they come to know him more fully.

A church is a true church only when it is the obedient agent and servant of Christ. Some churches make the mistake of becoming national churches, or preacher's churches, or racial churches. Other churches let someone other than Christ dominate them. Such churches as these soon cease to be Christian. They lose their power to witness to the gospel. Every church must be in constant touch with Christ and must obey his will. While no church can ever be perfectly Christian or fully obey Christ, all churches must constantly live and work in a spirit of repentance and loving obedience to him.

The relationship between Christ and the Church is indeed a mystery. Why should Christ use a human church as his agent? Why should he live in a human church? All we know is that he *does* live and work through the Church. It is his body. He does his divine work of saving men through this body. Through it he seeks to save the world, to announce, and to set up his Kingdom.

25

The Church is the home of Christ's Spirit

We have just seen how Christ depends on the Church to work out his will. The Church also depends on Christ. It depends on his presence to keep it alive and to give it direction and character.

The Church is constantly renewed and made more alive through the mind and heart and will of Christ. Its aim and its dynamic power derive from his person and ministry, and especially from his death, his resurrection, and his living presence in men's hearts today. Without him the Church soon degenerates into a society of good will or an ethical club.

The Church must be subject to its Head! Its purpose is to work for him and with him, and to do as he did when he was on earth. The Church has power, purpose, and persistence only when it is consciously and willingly aware of Christ's presence in it. Such a church will be saved from confusion and lack of integrity. It will be compelling in its witness, genuine in its worship, and warm in its fellowship. It will cultivate the mind of Christ. It will express his compassion. Its goals will become the goals he worked for in his ministry on earth. It will acquire a group conscience that is born of his righteousness.

When Christ is present in the Church, it will not only have a new kind of social life; it will also have a new group mind in the truth. Thoughts will become cleaner and clearer. Motives will become purer. Wills will have greater energy. Such a church becomes Christ's unique agent to redeem the world.

Our greatest need today is to renew the life of the Church. How can we do this? Some people think we should return to formal religion. Others say we need more educated and efficient leaders. Many feel we need a unity which will cement the churches into one strong Christian body. Still others insist we need a more educated church membership.

All these arguments have some merit, but they hardly touch the major issue. What we need most is a new sense of the commanding presence of Christ in our own lives and in the life of the Church. The need is for a greater consecration, a fuller surrender, and a truer allegiance to Christ. Only thus can the Church be saved and made into a power to save the world. Only when Christ lives among us personally will the Church be the body of Christ.

The Church in unity and diversity

One of the marvels of the body is its unity in diversity. All of its parts work together, and yet each one is different from the other. Just so, we find this unity in diversity in the Church. It is unified, yet it is made up of many different kinds of people. It includes people of all races, all nationalities, all ages, and of all conditions. It deals with them from birth to death, and it touches their lives at every crucial and critical period.

Like the body, it is a living unity under the direction of a person. It respects the differences in people, and yet it brings and holds them together in a living unity. It is this sense of unity in Christ as God and Saviour that is uniting churches in life and work and faith and order in recent times. Christians who believe in Jesus Christ feel that they are one in him, even though they belong to different churches and hold widely variant views on many items in the Christian faith. They are convinced that they belong to the body of Christ, although they have not yet found a way to express that unity fully. Yet, through various councils of churches, whether in the community,

27

nation, or the world, they are finding one another in a fellowship that becomes increasingly binding and meaningful.

What does the body of Christ imply?

We can easily see what the idea of the Church as the body of Christ implies. If the Church is a living reality with an organization, it is like a family. While it is an institution on earth, it is far more than that. A family is a fellowship of people who love and care for one another. They are bound together by more than formal ties. Each person feels keenly the hurts, the sorrows, and the joys that come to the rest of the family. So it is with the Church. What happens to one church member in any part of the world is felt by all. The minister is not the only one who should feel a concern for church members. All Christians should feel this concern for one another, for all are living members of the Body.

But deeper still, a church that regards itself as the body of Christ senses that it is a new creation in him and that it partakes of the very life of Christ himself. The Church is really united with Christ, and as such it becomes the new humanity originating with Christ, as the old humanity originated with Adam. The Church as his body participates in his dying and his rising again. Thus being united with him, Christians are united with one another. "In him," and Paul Minear says, "all families become one family, all nations one holy nation, all races one chosen race." To be members of the Church in truth is to be incorporated into that body which God through Christ is now building among all nations and is perfecting until all attain mature manhood—the measure of the stature of the fullness of Christ. The Church is the first fruit of all creation. To be sure, each member has differing gifts, but each is meant to develop his fullest potential and to enrich the whole community. To be a member of the body of Christ means to be crucified with him, raised with him, and united in him with all for whom he died.

If this be so, then the Church as the body of Christ will also be called upon to suffer for the world, give its life for the world, and be raised by the power of the Spirit continually so as to revive the life of the world. It cannot be absolved from the sacrifice which Christ, its head, suffered, if it is to be the body of the new humanity which its head is gathering from among all peoples.

The Church, then, as the body of Christ is God's way of restoring humanity, through Christ, to its true nature and destiny which it lost in Adam. The Church is the human race as God calls it to be and as it is becoming.

It is thus of the very nature of the Church that it has a mission to the whole world. That mission is our participation in the work of God which takes place between the coming of Jesus Christ to inaugurate God's Kingdom on earth, and His coming again in glory to bring that Kingdom to consummation. . . . Our work until His coming again is but the result of our share in the work which He is doing all the time and everywhere. The Church's mission is thus the most important thing that is happening in history.

CHAPTER THREE

THE PLACE OF COMMON WORSHIP

THE CHURCH IS THE COMMUNITY OF WORSHIP!

The delegates who met in the Amsterdam Assembly of the World Council of Churches could not decide whether the Church's chief aim was to proclaim the good news or to worship God. Many thought these were of equal importance.

Of course, the Church worships God! But it must not stop with worship. It must witness for him, too. It must witness in its worship, its fellowship, its acts of mercy, its education, its home life, and in the life and work of each member. If a church only worships, it may become ingrown, conservative, retrospective, and traditional. If a church only witnesses, it may become overactive. It may lose its form, its heritage, and its integrity. Worship is kept vital by witness, and witness is kept orderly by worship.

For centuries, Christians have worshiped in churches. They have sent up their corporate prayers and praises to God. The ancient songs of the Church have been voiced by more people than we could count. There has always been a sacred place where people gather for worship. In this place they have been still and known that God is God. They have confessed their sins and been forgiven. They have heard the Bible read and interpreted. They have remembered the mighty acts of God done for their redemption. They have prayed for themselves and for their fellow men. They have praised God in song and in word. They have dedicated their lives and their talents to him. They have received other people into their fellowship through confession and baptism. Together they have eaten the bread and drunk the wine of Holy Communion. They have given themselves anew in loyalty to God and in service to other people. And they have received a blessing before they parted, and have dispersed in the consciousness that they were still in the great company. We call this common, or united worship.

The nature of public worship

Nearly all men worship in one way or another. Every religion has its sacred places, its rules of discipline, its rituals, and its services. The Moslem worships in his mosque, the Hindu in his temple, the Shintoist at his shrine, and the Christian in his church.

Even the Nazis, who had little concern for the Christian Church, had to worship something; so their party became their church. Their mass meetings became their worship services. Their rally songs became their hymns. Their political doctrines became their dogmas. And their heroes became their saints. They worshiped a god of blood and soil and followed their "messiah" with blind and fanatical devotion. Communists also have their church, their worship, their creed, and their liturgy.

Man must worship something, even if it be himself, his country, the group to which he belongs, or the forces of nature. He is made for worship—for devotion. It lifts him up out of his littleness and sets him in a larger context. He becomes a part of something greater than he is. He puts value on something or someone—an act that

makes his life richer. When men share in this act of devotion, it is public worship in the broadest sense of the
word.

While all men worship, they do not all worship the
same thing or in the same way. There is a world of difference between worshiping God and worshiping Allah
or the gods of the Hindus. The meaning of worship is not
so much in *how* men do it, it is more in the *object* of their
devotion. Worship simply means "worthship." Christian
worship expresses the value or worth we put on the God
who is revealed in Jesus Christ. It is our response to the
God who has spoken and acted on our behalf. We could
not worship him in the right way if he had not made himself known to us through the Bible, and especially through
Christ.

As Henry Sloane Coffin has said, "Worship is adoration
of God, appreciation of God, delight in God, glorifying
God, enjoying God, communing with God, and offering
up ourselves to God." Christian worship takes place when
we acknowledge the Holy One before whom the whole
world must be silent. It takes place when we respond to the
heavenly Father who wants all men to accept his love
and live in obedience to his will.

When people truly worship, they do it in spirit and
in truth. They worship God in accordance with his character and his purpose. John Whale had the right idea when
he said a congregation at a church service is not a school
of people agreeing on correct doctrines, although Christianity does imply doctrine. It is a company of people who
express their belief in united communion with God. In
this kind of worship people say "Amen," or "Yea, verily,"
to God's call.

The elements of worship

People who have studied worship tell us we can find all the essential elements of public worship in the sixth chapter of Isaiah. True worship has a rhythm and a logic that we would do well to know and obey. If we are to approach God, we should approach him with the respect that is due his nature. When we approach the king of a nation, we must wear the right clothes and show the proper manner. Should we not have this same respect—and even more— for the King of kings?

Isaiah's vision in the temple indicates some important stages through which we go in our worship. First, he was in the mood for worship. Evidently he was discouraged, lonely, and in need of help. He needed God, and the temple was the place where he expected to find him. He remembered the year he had his vision, for King Uzziah's death must have affected him greatly. We worship rightly when we go to church in a mood of inquiry, expectancy, gratitude, and faith.

Second, Isaiah saw the Lord "high and lifted up." The Lord sat on a throne, and his train filled the temple. His ministering spirits, the seraphim, adored him as the Holy One. His glory filled the earth. Isaiah saw his greatness and his glory. He saw that God is all-powerful and ever-present. If we would worship right, we must see God.

Third, Isaiah became aware of his own sin and his involvement in the sin of the people of his time. He became humble, and he cried, "Woe is me!" When the glory of God is seen, the ingloriousness of life is exposed. When men see God's high calling for them, they see how low their living is. Life needs cleansing and forgiveness.

Fourth, Isaiah was forgiven. He did not deny his faults, hide them, or blame them on somebody else. He confessed them, and God forgave him. And forgiveness is from above and from the altar. God's everlasting mercy alone can offer us real forgiveness of sin.

Fifth, no sooner had Isaiah been forgiven than he heard a voice inquire, "Who will go for us?" He could not avoid the voice of God. For when he received grace, he was made aware of his high obligation to God and his responsibility to his people and generation.

Isaiah found no rest until he moved into the sixth stage of worship—dedication. His response to all he had seen and felt was, "Here am I; send me." He offered his whole life as a witness and a service to God. Though Isaiah faced a wicked and difficult world, God told him to go and do what he saw as his duty, whether or not people would listen to him or accept his help. Come what may, he must have hope and do what he was called to do.

Most of our worship services include these elements: prelude, call to worship, invocation, confession, declaration of forgiveness, Gloria Patri, scripture reading, offering, group prayer, sermon, and benediction. In his booklet *Learning to Worship,* Boynton Merrill gives a Bible passage to interpret each element in the service:

On Entering: "Be still and know that I am God."

The Prelude: "While I mused, the fire burned."

The Call to Worship: "Holy, Holy, Holy," or "Bless the Lord, O my Soul—Forget not."

The Invocation: "Draw nigh to us, as we draw nigh . . ."

The Confession: "All we like lost sheep have gone astray."

The Declaration of Forgiveness: "As far as the east is from the west . . ." or "With him there is plenteous redemption."

The Gloria: "Rejoice always, and again I say, rejoice."

The Scripture: "Did not our hearts burn?"

The Offering: "Every good and perfect gift," or "Such as I have give I."

The Prayers: "Let us, therefore, come boldly," or "Praying always."

The Sermon: "Thus saith the Lord." [Surely if every sermon were tested over against that text, all of them would be preached more humbly, and many would never be preached at all.]

The Benediction: "The peace of God," or "The grace of our Lord Jesus Christ."

A church may have an ideal form, the most learned minister, and the loveliest cathedral in which to worship; but if it lacks the right spirit, its worship lacks reality. Good form, learned preaching, and interesting services are not enough. God waits to enter into a communion with his children. He has established ways by which he makes himself known to men. But people who come to God must believe that he is, that he cares for them, and that he reveals himself, if they are to worship truly. They must make the human element transparent so that the truth may shine through. They must make ready to receive their gracious Host.

The sacraments in worship

According to evangelical Christianity the two major elements in worship are 1) preaching the Word of God and 2) observing the sacraments.

The gospel is to be preached, heard, and believed. When a man really preaches, he brings God's Word to bear on people's lives. He proclaims God's action to redeem man. He sounds forth the good news that is the grand theme of the Bible. He lifts up Christ, who is the way, the truth, the life, the judge, the redeemer, and the hope of man. He bases his sermon on the great theme of redemption. In it he deals with the central and crucial figure of Jesus Christ, in whose manhood and ministry and mandate God has made direct contact with men. Through his teachings, ministry, death, and resurrection, God became real to men. Through him God sounded forth his authority over men. Through him men can have victory over death and hell. This kind of sermon is not the opinion of a man. It is an earnest proclamation of the eternal Word by a minister of Christ. Real preaching is sacramental; it is the unique means of bringing God to men. The preacher is a herald of God, beseeching men to listen to the claims of God in Christ, to engage in self-examination, to repent, to believe the gospel, and to obey God. Real preaching is more than words; it is the way by which God wrestles with persons to meet them in face-to-face encounter and conversation. The gospel and preaching go together.

The Lord's Supper has always been the inmost sanctuary of our whole Christian worship. Down through the centuries and across the earth it has been the mark that distinguishes the Christian Church. At the Lord's Supper men remember the sacrificial act of Jesus for all men. As they remember and take the bread and the cup, through faith, they partake of the given mercy of God in Christ. What happened years ago on Calvary becomes as real as though it were happening today. As we nourish our bodies by daily food and drink, so we nourish our spirits by partaking of all that is in Christ in humble faith. Everything we need is given to us by God. At the Lord's Supper we acknowledge that we live by his providence and grace. At his command we eat and drink together. We have communion with God and communion with one another through this *act* of worship.

Baptism, like the Lord's Supper, is an essential form of worship, a visible word, an "outward and visible sign of an inner and spiritual grace." Baptism and the Lord's Supper are the two sacraments observed in Protestant churches.

People are baptized when they become members of a church. Water is used for cleansing. In the church it is used as the sign of the cleansing of man's spirit by the grace of God. Different churches have different forms of baptism. Some immerse adult believers only. As such it is a confession of faith, and a sign that they have been buried and raised with Christ. Other churches baptize infants, not as a confession of the infants' faith, but as a sign that they are included in the community of Christ, that they can receive God's grace even though they are mere infants, and that they are included in the covenant community of Christ. They are entitled to all the rights and privileges of God's children. Their faith begins in the bosom of the Church. When we baptize our babies, however, we become responsible to nurture them faithfully so that later on they will confirm the Church's faith by a personal profession. God does his part. We must respond with serious training.

The effects of worship

The effects of true worship are many and varied. Of course when men worship God in spirit and in truth, they do not think of how it will affect them or our world. Men do not go to church to *use* God for their own ends. They go so that he can use them for his purposes. Men do not adjust God to their world. They adjust their world to

37

God. They worship him for his own sake and not for what they can get out of him. An effect of true worship is that it changes one's present way of life and turns him to God. People who truly worship God in church bring their world to church with them, lift it up to God in penitence and prayer, and dedicate it to him.

Worship sets men free from themselves and from the things of the world. It sets men's lives within the framework of God's eternal purpose. It brings them into fellowship with kindred spirits who encourage and bulwark them in the conflicts of life. It shuts out the noise of the world, so they can reflect upon God and listen to his voice. It puts them in touch with the ancient wisdom that cleanses, guides and stimulates the mind. It unites them with the communion of saints of all ages.

Worship softens the heart, expands the horizon of thought, and deepens the insight. It sets men free from anxiety and fear as they see their lives made strong by the everlasting arms of a faithful God. It inspires holy imagination. It enhances the smallness of life and fills it with the grandeur becoming the children of a heavenly Father. It unites men in a new devotion to God. It stirs them to action by filling them with a fresh sense of the holy mission and the high calling of human life. The person who is "lost in wonder, love, and praise" finds his life renewed as he gives himself to his Creator. Laying in "dust life's glory dead," he finds that "from the ground there blossoms red life that shall endless be." But best of all, true worship unites men with God in a personal way, and it unites men with each other for time and for eternity in a bond that cannot be dissolved.

It is little wonder then that worship is our major privilege and duty in the Church. Without it everything—

education, evangelism, service, fellowship—would lack the essential element. Worship is the very spirit of everything that is done in the Church.

True group worship is necessary in the life of every Christian. It is not a matter of choice. In fact, one cannot have a well-developed Christian life without it. It is in church that men really learn to pray. It is in worshiping together that they learn what worship means. To habitually stay away from church brings disaster to the personal devotional life of the Christian.

True worship has more than a personal effect. It has a powerful social influence. If whole communities would worship in the true spirit, one could think of nothing more powerful toward bringing peace on earth or making the social order reverent. When all men worship God in church and in their daily lives together, all life will be sacramental.

The principles of worship

Church worship involves definite principles. In worship men cannot do as they please. They must observe certain rules to worship God right. While we may worship him anywhere, at any time, in different postures, and in any dress, we cannot worship him unless we fulfill certain spiritual requirements. God must be worshiped in accordance with his character—that is, in spirit and in truth.

To worship truly men must be humble, faithful, sincere, and love their fellow men. The proud, self-sufficient, unbelieving person simply cannot worship God. The prophets of the Old Testament preached with vigor against the "temple worship" of people who merely went through the motions of worship. Jesus warned people against showing their religion outwardly, when they are not sincere in their hearts. It is better, he said, for the worshiper to leave his gift and first be reconciled to his brother before he offers it in the sanctuary. He cautioned his followers against allowing religious forms to become a substitute for inner piety. He did not imply that formal worship is of no value; nor did the prophets suggest that people substitute personal worship for group worship. Both Jesus and the prophets called on people to worship God honestly. Outward morality and church ritual are not a substitute for sincerity in the heart.

The first principle of true worship is the deep consciousness of the worshiper that God is of the greatest importance, that he is real, that he is present with him, and that he is always available. Worship is not something that can be worked up. Lively music, ecstatic oratory, or group spirit is not true worship. All of these may arouse enthusiasm, but enthusiasm is not necessarily worship. Men worship truly when they respond to God, who gives and reveals himself to them through his Word. The spirit of worship must be awakened by something outside ourselves. God comes to us, and our response to him is the beginning and the end of worship. We must be careful not to try to produce worship by "getting up" worship programs for the sake of a lively and inspiring service. Rather, worship must come from God's love for man. Anything else is certainly not the true worship of God.

If common worship is to take place, one man or one group must not dominate the service. In some churches the minister is too conspicuous. He leads the worship. The gifted preacher, especially, must be careful not to make the worship center in himself—his voice or his person—so the church becomes his church alone. No matter how well trained he is to speak and to lead, he may hinder his congregation from worshiping God if he intrudes himself too strongly into the service. He may even regard everything else as preliminary or incidental to his sermon. But the sermon is only one part of the worship service—and not even the most important part.

Worship must never become entertainment. That great Danish Christian of the last century, Sören Kierkegaard, noticed the tendency of the people in his day to go to church in the same spirit they went to the theater. They went to be entertained. They regarded the minister and the choir as the actors providing the entertainment. It repels us to think of people using a church for this purpose when they ought to be waiting upon their royal Lord. All churches would do well to think about the ways they worship lest the service become only a program or an activity. Nothing would be worse for our world than that people going to church to meet God should see his holiness broken down by a lack of reverence. Disaster comes to personality and to society when the church treats God lightly.

We cannot make up our forms of worship on the spur of the moment. While we must allow freedom for the Holy Spirit to act, men cannot worship God in a haphazard manner. People have been worshiping in churches for centuries, and during that time they have developed wise habits of worship. These habits, hallowed with age, are made binding by continued use. All denominations have their books of worship which preserve these forms. These forms should be used as much as possible in our common worship—if not literally, at least as guides. They have in them all the elements of true worship. It is high time churches stop making up and "improving" their worship services so often and learn to value more highly what the Holy Spirit has taught men in the past. No one who wishes to write poetry would begin without studying the poetry that has already been written. No one would venture to make up his own rules of social etiquette when the basic rules are already established. So why should we make up our own rules of worship etiquette as we please? Let there be freedom, but let that freedom be in the truth and love of Christ! In worship, we need to guard against both sheer individualism and rigid formalism.

When we abide by the principles of true worship, we should seek to make the architecture of our church conform to these principles. Sometimes, worship takes place under conditions that are not favorable. We can worship in a home, in a school, in the open air, or even in prison. But normally we should worship in a sanctuary properly furnished and in harmony with our Christian faith. We are building more and more churches that are worshipful in character. Yet many more could have the principles of beauty and dignity applied with good results. A house of worship without dignity is a sin against God and man.

The social nature of worship

The Lord is in His holy temple:
Let all the earth keep silence before Him.

When we say these solemn words, our spirits are hushed into silent wonder, reverence, and humility. The whole earth is bidden to stand in awe of the glory of the One who created all things and constantly sustains them. There is a throne at the center of things. It is the source of all being, all power, and all good. The universe is not a jumble of things without meaning. It is an orderly whole and an expression of God's purpose. In God all things

42

have meaning, and when we worship him, our lives becomes filled with meaning.

When Christians come together to worship God, their
common worship is a social act of the highest significance.
They are a part of the great company who acknowledge
God to be their Lord. The common worship of God is a
social reality written deep in cultures and in history.
When people worship one God, and stand before him in
common adoration and praise, they form a community
bound together by one of the strongest bonds known to
men. To worship a God of truth and love creates a people
who have his character. People become like the God they
worship.

We cannot confine this kind of worship to the Church.
It spreads throughout the whole community. It creates
the spirit of worship in our lives and our work, in our
homes and our schools. All life is created to be worshipful. When God's plan for the world becomes complete,
it will bring with it the fulfillment of church worship in
a new world where there will be no church, for all life
will have become reverent. Worship should not take place
apart from our daily life but in it. It should make daily
life holy.

All the elements of common worship are social. With
their fellow men, worshipers are caught up in a group
relationship to God. The general confession in the worship service is intended to make men conscious of their
common sins. "We have offended against Thy holy laws,"
they pray. Thus they acknowledge their common guilt
and confess their common sins before God.

The pastoral prayer is offered by the minister *for* the
people of this church and community. It includes all of
their petitions and thanksgivings. In worship no minister

can pray for himself alone. He must be one with his people. The Lord's Prayer is a group prayer. It starts with the word "our." God is *our* Father. We ask God to give us *our* daily bread. We pray for the forgiveness of *our* debts, or trespasses. We ask God to lead *us* not into temptation, but to deliver *us* from evil. In prayer, men confess that they belong to one another and that their lives are tightly bound together in guilt as well as in forgiveness, in dependence on God to guide them as well as to deliver them. All need the support of his fatherhood, his heavenly nature, his will, and his kingdom. In prayer, they are also united with people outside the church, even though those outside do not admit they need God or constantly depend on him.

In true worship, all men are our brothers. To pray for all conditions of men, is to pray for those who are sick and in trouble, for those who are not saved, and those who are oppressed—for all peoples and their rulers. Thus to pray is to make the needs of all men one's own.

The offering is a group act of worshipful giving. Through the offering, it is acknowledged that money and goods are a trust from God, to be used as a trust and to be shared with those in need.

To sing the great hymns of the Church is to take part in a social act, in the Church's unending song. When men truly sing the words as well as the melody, they become aware not only of the personal devotion of the men who wrote the hymns, but also of the devotion of all Christians who glorify God through them.

The social nature of worship is most evident in the Sacraments. Baptism is more than a personal matter. It is a public initiation and concerns not only the person who is baptized but also his parents and relatives, and the

44

people in the congregation. And as men take part in the Lord's Supper, they become aware of their relationship to one another. They are reminded that their daily bread is a gift from God. All over the world the people who take part in the Supper become members together of the universal Church. After the Supper they pray to continue in holy fellowship with one another and to obey God in their lives.

William Temple regarded public worship as essential to the solution of all our social problems. When men gather together to worship, they take part in a social act. From the invocation to the benediction they speak for all men before God. The invocation reminds us of the God who creates our lives. The benediction dismisses us with the words that we are never out of his care and that we may continue in holy fellowship with one another after we leave the service.

CHAPTER FOUR

THE HERALD OF THE GOSPEL

THE CHURCH IS THE HERALD OF THE GOSPEL OF GOD!

The Church exists today because of some very important events that took place in history. These events are recorded in our Bible. They center in Jesus Christ—his coming into the world, his life and ministry, his death and resurrection, and his presence in the Church, in lives, and in history. We call these events and what they mean, the good news or the gospel. The news of God's saving acts for all men is the greatest news the world will ever hear!

The Church is made up of people who have heard this good news, responded to it, and now live in its truth and by its power. The Church is the herald, or witness, of this good news. Its primary task is to hear the gospel and to make the gospel known to all men.

In ancient Greece the Athenians and Persians were fighting a terrific battle on the plains of Marathon. The people of Athens waited anxiously for the outcome. Great issues were at stake as two mighty world powers fought in a life and death struggle. The moment victory seemed certain, a runner was sent to carry the word from Marathon to Athens. He ran swiftly without stopping to rest. His body was strained to the utmost. As he neared Athens, people hailed him from the walls of the city. For this meant that victory was won; the enemy was routed. There was hilarious rejoicing. This old story never fails to stir us. Here is the spirit of a herald who comes with good news, and the effect of this good news on a people who have been set free from tyranny.

In the Greco-Roman world, it was good news when a royal son was born, a king enthroned, or an enemy defeated. The gospel announces the birth of God's Son to rule, the enthronement of Christ the King, the inauguration of his kingdom, and the defeat of man's greatest enemy.

The gospel is the good news of a great victory for all men. It frees them from the power of sin and evil. It brings them the assurance and means of a new life. Always, the Church is the herald proclaiming this good news.

The primary task of the whole Church

The Church's first responsibility is to hear this good news again and again so that it may know it more fully. Faith comes by hearing the gospel preached and taught and sung. It must hear before it can be a church and witness to the gospel. After hearing it must use every means possible to bring the good news to all men. This is not the business of ministers and missionaries only. It is the business of every Christian—and of the whole church. Every Christian is a missionary, an ambassador, a witness. True, the minister is the spokesman for all. He is the Church's authorized herald of the gospel, and his words should express the spirit and the urgency of its message, but he is not the only witness. All the members of the Church should witness in and through their daily work, their homes, and their relationships. When they do, the Church becomes effective and wields great power. It becomes a Christianizing force in the community. Too many churches confine the task of witnessing to the minister and a few other people. Preaching, or witnessing, is the duty and privilege of every Christian. Such preaching can be done in many ways and in various places.

There is no Christianity without the gospel. Christians are marked by a spirit of joy and gratitude as well as by a spirit of urgency and enthusiasm in spreading the good news. Paul said, "Woe is unto me, if I preach not the gospel." One time when he was on trial, he said to a high Roman official who had ridiculed his enthusiasm for the gospel, "I am not mad. . . . I would to God, that not only thou, but also all that hear me this day, were . . . such as I am." These are the words of a man who had heard the good news, responded to it in obedient faith, and made it his life's business to pass it on to other men. A true Christian and a true church must have the missionary spirit. Indeed, the Church is a missionary society! Christianity without a gospel would have no passion, no deep joy, and no mighty urge to communicate itself to others.

The eternal gospel

We call the heart of the Christian faith the "eternal gospel." It is not dated; it is not confined to time or place. It is the gift of God. It has to do with our origin, our nature, our remaking, our vocation, and our destiny. As the late Archbishop Temple said, "The Gospel is true always and everywhere, or it is not a Gospel at all, or true at all."

Most people have the wrong idea about eternity. Some think of it as that which comes after death. Others think it is time continued without end. Rather, eternal refers to a state of being. It is a quality or a dimension. The gospel is eternal because it is not affected by time or by space. Yet, it comes to men in history and through persons. The gospel is for all men, for time and for eternity, for history and beyond history. It is the same yesterday, today, and forever.

If a scientist should discover the secret of cancer and find a sure cure for it, a sigh of relief would go up from all mankind. The people who have cancer would shout for joy. The people who have not had it could look to the future without the dread of it. The cure for cancer would be good news indeed! But it would be good news only for this world, good news affecting only the bodies of men. The eternal gospel is good news, too. It is good news of a special kind. It announces the defeat of evil and the forgiveness of sin. It makes available to men the power to overcome death. It proclaims an eternal power to meet a disease far worse than cancer. The gospel declares that men are not in the hands of a blind fate or unmerciful power, but of a just and merciful God. When men know this gospel for themselves, they will say with Paul, "Thanks be unto God for his unspeakable gift."

Good news about God

The gospel is a revelation—that is, it reveals, or uncovers the true nature of God and of man. It exposes God's character and purpose. As such it meets man's deepest need. All men seek to know the mystery of life. They want to know what it means. All religions try to give an answer to this never-ending quest. Christian people believe the gospel reveals God within the range of man's understanding and brings the living God within the range of human appropriation. It offers saving knowledge of the mystery of God and man. The gospel does not tell us everything about everything, but it does tell us what we need to know to find the real meaning of life.

The gospel tells us that in the beginning God was, that he is now, and that he always will be. "In him we live, and move, and have our being." He is a personal being whose wisdom has created all things and whose power sustains all things. His nature is love, and his will is good, true, just, and righteous. His purpose is directed toward the well-being of his children. The environment as well as the origin and goal of life is in the God who is righteous, true, and merciful. The environment and ground of all existence is good and faithful.

Good news about our salvation

We must always see the good news of God against the background of the bad news of man. God created man in his own image and gave him freedom and rule over the earth. Man bears a kinship to God, and God meant him to live in fellowship with his Creator and with his neighbors. But he rebelled against God. He took things into his own hands. He put himself above God; indeed, he put himself and other things in the place of God. He worshiped creations of his own hand and mind, and upset the way of life God had intended for him. The result is tragedy for man's personal and social life. He is lost. He lives under God's displeasure. What was meant to be a paradise is closed by the flaming sword of God's judgement. Man is not what he was created to be. He is a compound of a God-made and a self-made creature. He lives a dual life.

All men are alike. They play God. They do as they please. They accept God's good gifts without gratitude.

They act like the prodigal son, who demanded that his father give him the goods that belonged to him. This is the way of individual men, groups of men, and nations of men. It is the way of the world. Men put themselves at the center of things—even at the center of religion. They even run the Church. They use God for their own ends. They are proud—even of their faith and their humility. Of course, they are not as bad as they might be, but they are persistent and constant sinners. They miss the mark of their divine calling and destiny. They fill the earth with their ungodly living.

But they cannot get away with it! There is a law that catches up with them sooner or later. It is not natural for men to live without order. It is God's judgment on their false way of life. God does not will their destruction, but he will not be mocked. He sets bounds to sin and to evil. Whatever a man sows, that he is bound to reap. Men may resist God, but they resist in vain. They only harm themselves. When they take life into their own hands, they go against God's plan for them.

The glory of the gospel is that God does not leave man to his fate. Even in his rebellion man dimly senses that he is resisting something he ought to be. God still bounds man's sinfulness by his correcting love and his fatherly care. He treats us like unruly children. He wants us to choose his way freely and willingly. His dealing with us is "true and righteous, altogether." God's power is always controlled by his love. The marvelous truth about his judgment on us is that he never forsakes us or disowns us. He tempers his judgment with mercy, and with his love seeks to draw us to himself. He does not sit in his heaven with no interest in our fate. He takes the first step in

51

rescuing us from our despair, our loneliness, and our guilt. At the Madras Missionary Conference of 1938 it was said:

God in His infinite love has acted for man's salvation. He has come among them in Jesus of Nazareth, His Word made flesh. In him, He has conquered the power of sin and death. Jesus Christ in His teachings and life of perfect love recalls men to that which God would have them be, and brings them to shame for their betrayal of His expectation. . . . In the strength and joy of forgiveness, daily renewed at the foot of the cross, they are made more than conquerors over every evil.

This is the good news: While we were still sinners, Christ visited us, ministered to us, suffered for us, and overcame the power of death and of hell for us. Because this is so, we may be forgiven, healed, and restored. This is why the New Testament rings with joy. God has acted finally, dramatically, and crucially! The gates of new life are open to those with an humble and a seeking heart.

The gospel is good news about the future. Those who are risen with Christ have the hope of eternal life. They have passed from death into life. They share the risen life of Christ, who was dead and is now alive forever. Eternal life cannot be destroyed by death. The resurrection of Jesus Christ is the assurance of the resurrection of all believers. Death has lost its power and its sting. To have eternal life does not mean simply that men go on living after death. Death is not the end of our futile and disappointing existence. Rather, it is the gateway into fulness of life to those who know the new life in Christ. Through his power God draws men to him, and they become what he has always wanted them to be. "As many as received him, to them gave he power to become the sons of God."

Good news about the kingdom of God

The gospel is good news about the kingdom of God. Through Christ the Kingdom came upon all men. It is now open to all believers. Jesus brought God's new order among men. The kingdom of God is evident in Israel, to be sure. But Jesus brought the Kingdom in his person and advent. Through him something new has been added to the historical processes. He was the turning point in history. When people respond to God in Christ and accept him as their Lord and Savior, they enter the Kingdom. God has always ruled this rebellious world, and there have always been faithful souls who believed in him. But it was not until Jesus came that people saw the Kingdom in a person. Jesus is the center of that Kingdom.

The Kingdom is the hope of the future, as well as the inspiration of the present. It is the real world set in this false world. In it the true order of creation is restored, and relationships that have been destroyed by sin are in process of restoration and renewal. The coming of the Kingdom gives us reason to rejoice. It is not visible but there are signs of the reality of its presence and coming everywhere. The promise of its consummation is the basis of our hope for the future and our source of Christian action.

No wonder Jesus called the Kingdom man's highest good! We must seek it first of all. We must seek it as a merchant seeks a valuable pearl. That we may enter this kingdom is good news. We cannot buy membership in it; nor can we enter it through intellectual, moral, or aesthetic achievements. The qualities we need to enter the Kingdom are humility, self-criticism, trust and obedience. (See the Sermon on the Mount.) Would that people could see the kingdom of God as life's greatest value! Then they would think of repentance and faith as privileges rather than as burdens.

Good news about the goal of history

The gospel is also good news about the meaning of history. Man's long story seems to have no plan or reason; but to the Christian, history is the plane on which God is working out his grand design. History does not go round and round in endless cycles that mean nothing and get nowhere. Nor is it a nice story of inevitable progress toward an inevitable Utopia to be inherited by the people who have the good fortune to be alive when it appears. History is the stage on which God is bringing to pass his grand purpose. History moves toward an end, a goal; it is a process of judgment and mercy.

Does this mean that evil will be overcome in history and in time may even disappear from the earth? We believe evil will finally be destroyed. We do not know why evil came into a world created by a loving Father. But we do know that through the power of Christ it has been overcome and that we may live as conquerors of evil in this world. We know, too, that evil has no life of its own. It is real, but it is a parasite that lives off the good. Evil also has within it the seeds of its own destruction. Evil people consume each other, as do evil nations. This is the law of God. God alone can destroy evil. But we can overcome it in our hearts through faith and love.

So, though evil is real, it is judged by God and by his saints. God did not create evil. It is permitted in his world; it is a mystery. And we will have to contend with it to the end of history. Jesus Christ the Lord has overcome evil in principle; the complete triumph is yet to come. In the meantime, the holy warfare continues. Since Jesus died on the cross and triumphed over evil, it is on the defensive. Even though we are still constantly threatened by it, we live and work in the power of the Easter triumph and the future hope. That hope has been called the "oxygen" of man's life; without it, he would soon suffocate and die.

Just how and when the final victory over evil will take place is shrouded in mystery. We know it will come, but it waits upon God's free action. We may trust him to bring it to pass in his own time and in his own way. Even now God's judgments are in evidence. History will come to an end. Everything that is not in harmony with God's purpose will be destroyed, and God will be all in all.

The spirit of the herald

If a church knows the gospel, it will be eager to tell it to the world. This news is so important that the Church cannot keep quiet about it. It will speak with authority and will keep on finding new and relevant ways to reach men with its message. It will not bring the gospel to just a few or to certain people. It will take the Gospel to everyone, regardless of his social standing, nationality, or race. It will make the gospel plain. It will witness in the spirit of love and concern. It will not merely preach pious words from a pulpit. It will pass on the good news by personal testimony, daily life, and by identifying love for the neighbors. As the gospel was brought to us, so the Church will bring the gospel to others.

The spirit of the good news should enter into everything the Church says and does. The Church should have about it the spirit of Pentecost. It should draw men by the vitality and dynamic power of its fellowship. The world will then be made aware of a people in it who express the life-giving news from God. The Church with such a message will be a church that is heard and felt. It will attract people by the sincerity and purity of its life.

A Christian church must be more concerned about its message than about itself. It must regard itself as trusted with the precious gospel. It will not be afraid of men. It will be done with the spirit of futility and defeat.

The church has urgent and liberating news to get through to men. But all too often it tells this news in dull ways. There can be no genuine revival of Christianity until our churches experience the gospel. A new reformation is needed! A philosophy of religion or a code of ethics is not a gospel. We are not communicating the *gospel* when we tell people to be good, to support the Church, or to make the world a better place in which to live.

The good news is that there is a living God who is the Father Almighty. He redeems people through Jesus Christ. He forgives them, and he offers them the power of a new life through the Holy Spirit. He makes all things new. His purpose cannot be thwarted. He works recreatively in and through people who repent and believe. The Kingdom is a sure reality, it is at work in history, and it is coming.

The field is the world

The gospel is for the whole world. A church that knows the gospel sends missionaries or fraternal workers to other lands. The story of missions is one of the most exciting in history. Because of the missionary thrust at the heart of the gospel, churches have been set up in nearly every nation. Many of the younger churches have become full-grown and independent. They are developing their own institutions, sending out their own missionaries, becoming Christian forces in society, and supporting themselves. We are living in a new era of missionary history. We must offer help to the younger churches so that they may become mature and take their places as equals and partners among the older churches. As heralds of the gospel, churches must become more united so that they may become more effective witnesses for Christ to the world.

But the field of the world is not only out there among the nations, but in the whole world of human life and relationships. It is in the deeper reaches of human motivation. A mission field is any area of personal or corporate life which is not under the complete lordship of Jesus Christ. The Church must proclaim the gospel to all creatures and to the end of history.

CHAPTER FIVE

THE SCHOOL OF PERSONAL CHRISTIANITY

THE CHURCH IS THE SCHOOL OF CHRISTIAN NURTURE! The Church is the place or community where personal Christianity starts and grows. It is the school God planned to bring persons into a relationship with himself, and into a communal relationship with one another.

Education is one of the great concerns of mankind. Today it has become a matter of heated debate. Criticisms are being directed against the present educational system because it fails to provide an adequate education of individuals in this kind of world. Regardless as to the arguments which are offered pro and con, the present discussion is concerned with the nature and purpose of education. What are the objectives of education? How shall these objectives be accomplished? What are the essential elements which must be included in our educational philosophy? All of these questions go back ultimately to deeper questions: What is the nature of man? For what is he to be educated? What are the objectives of life, personally and socially, which education should seek to develop? Education, it is easy to see, deals with the profoundest realities of man's nature.

The Old Testament school

It has been maintained that the Old Testament describes Israel as a nurturing community. Education was not confined so much to schools and other educational institutions; rather, the whole community educated its children, youth, and adults. The home and the tribe were the primary nuturing agencies. But the whole nation was a close-knit community which was founded upon a definite curriculum. That curriculum was the mighty acts of God by which he had created this unique people. The Law was the core of that curriculum, for it declared the basic foundation of God's people. The feast days, celebration, and rites of worship in the tabernacle and temple were dramatic teaching means in which young and old participated meaningfully in the history, nature, and mission of the people. Always these covenant people were aware of the fact that they did not create themselves; they were called out from among the nations, they were delivered by mighty acts of God, and they were a people of a mission and destiny.

There was no distinction made between religious and secular education, because all life was regarded as God-given and God-directed. All work was God's work. Religion was integral to home life. Every phase of life was related to God and his holy purpose. Even the land was called holy, for it was a gift of God and its fertility was divinely given. Mountains and valleys and deserts bore religious names for they were associated with God's relation to the people.

In this nation-school, parents, particularly the father, were the primary teachers and the home was the religious community set within the covenant nation. To be sure, there were designated leaders who were teachers as well, especially the priests who, by ceremonial laws, regulated life from sickness to marriage. The prophets became Israel's greatest teachers, for they provided a deeper interpretation of God's purpose for the nation and her mission among the nations. Prophets were given the gift of interpreting God's ways with men. They were fearless preachers of righteousness, recalling Israel time and again to an obedience to God and his mission for her. Several of them became so identified with the nation in its rebellion and defection that they suffered physically and spiritually for Israel, thus pointing to the vicious nature of Israel's sin which could be overcome only through vicarious sacrifice. The prophets were Israel's—and mankind's—greatest teachers.

After the Exile, much that was oral and dramatic in Israel's education became literary and liturgical and legalistic. Sensing what disaster could do to the nation, the people exalted the office of rabbi and with it the synagogue and rabbinical schools. Israel has always been highly literate and eagerly interested in education.

The Christian Church had its origin in the bosom of a nurturing nation. Jesus was called rabbi. Much of the gospel is devoted to his teachings. The Christian faith is based upon the truth which is meant to illuminate the mind, to set it free from error and superstition, and to throw the light of God upon the whole life of man. A Christian Church that is not a school is hardly Christian.

Jesus and the school

Jesus gathered people into a fellowship around him and kept them with him during his life on earth. They heard him speak. They watched him at work. They asked him questions. He educated them gradually to take over his ministry. Jesus was the teacher of this fellowship, or informal school. It had neither books, organization, nor equipment, but it was a school in the best sense of the word. It was a holy association of his disciples or learners, united in his person, teachings, and purpose. Jesus demonstrated his love not only in his personal concern for his disciples, but also in his death on the cross for them. After he died, was raised from the grave, and ascended into heaven, his school was blessed by the presence of the Holy Spirit. The Holy Spirit is the inward teacher of man's spirit, who interprets what Jesus said and did. Christian education is almost a sacrament when it is carried on in the spirit of Christ in the fellowship of the Church.

G. R. H. Shafto, in his little book *The School of Jesus,* says that the methods Jesus used as a teacher were (1) companionship, (2) friendship, and (3) encouragement. He did not teach merely in a formal way. His disciples *lived* with him. Jesus meant them to be like him. He wanted his joy to be in them. Someone has said that one third of the parables were addressed to them. He performed some of his miracles for their benefit. Through this transforming friendship with Jesus these ordinary men were educated into becoming sons of God. Jesus placed his supreme emphasis on this companionship. To be in the school of Jesus meant to live with him.

Jesus spoke of his students as friends. He lived with them and shared in their daily lives. He spoke to them as children, as little ones. The late scholar T. R. Glover made bold to say Jesus referred to his disciples as boys. There was a casual intimacy between Jesus and his students. Adolf Harnack has coined a happy phrase that illustrates this spirit of Jesus' school, "infinite love in ordinary intercourse."

61

Jesus' school was filled with the spirit of encouragement. He believed in his students. He expected great things of them. He entrusted them with great responsibilities. He called them the "salt of the earth" and the "light of the world." Although at times they failed him miserably he still trusted them and prayed for them. He loved his own unto the end. They were to him as brother and sister and mother. Unpromising as they seemed, he prayed that they might be made stronger. When he left them, he entrusted his cause to their care.

This intimate little company of people around Jesus was the beginning of the Church. What it was in the days of Jesus, it is still meant to be—a recruiting agency attracting men to discipleship with Jesus, and a nurturing school for the perfecting or maturing of the saints.

The Church brings in disciples

How do people become Christians? No one is born a Christian. No one inherits Christianity biologically from his parents. There is no direct way to become a Christian without some contact with other Christians. You cannot make up your own faith. Nor can you normally become a Christian by coming into direct contact with Christ. You must come in contact with a Bible, a Christian or a group of Christians, a Christian hospital or institution, or Christian literature. The Church is your teacher. It has kept alive the memory of Jesus Christ, who lived in Palestine years ago. It organizes its life around him in its worship, its fellowship, its education, and its charity. One becomes a Christian by making contact in one way or another with the Church. Cyprian, an early church father, said that "outside the church there is no salvation." Calvin said that whoever has God for his Father has the Church for his mother.

Some people grow up in the Church, others are won to its membership. In some churches children whose parents are church members are baptized or dedicated in infancy. They make up a group of people who are oriented toward God and surrounded by, steeped in, and influenced by his Spirit from birth. They have a potentially Christian future. So, many churches regard children as members of the Church, though the children themselves have not chosen to be Christians. In short, the appeal of the Gospel comes early to children who are born into a Christian community. It comes to them in many ways—through their homes, through the influence of their parents, through Bible stories, through fellowship with Christian people, or through Sunday school and church. Children who have been baptized are carefully taught so that they may know what it means to believe in Christ and to become responsible church members. They take personal vows and are confirmed, or profess their faith in public at the age of discretion. Most church members become Christians by growing up in the Church. By passing through a process of education, they pass from stage to stage into the fully committed Christian life.

The dangers in this type of gradual growth are many. Many children grow up in the Church in a normal way. They are decent and law-abiding people. They support the Church and are its loyal friends. But often they are not properly taught to understand what it means to be living church members. They may be formal members of the Church, but they have not made the definite decision to become active, willing disciples of Jesus. Right here lies the danger in the old-line formal churches. They may have excellent traditions, but they do not practice a radical evangelism. Evangelism is essential in every church.

People born in the United States are American citizens. But they need an education to make them want to be Americans. If this education does not take place, our land will be filled with people who are Americans in name but not in truth. This same principle applies to the Church. The fact that someone is born into the Church is not a guarantee that he will become a Christian.

People who were not born into the Church are won to it in one way or another. This is a form of evangelism. These people may be brought into contact with Christ through a friend, through hearing a sermon, through visiting a church service, through reading a religious book, through a revival meeting, or through the help of a Christian in a time of crisis. Evangelism today uses both old and new ways to bring men and women to Christ. Sometimes a preacher or a team of preachers do the work. Sometimes trained Christians visit people who are not members of the Church. Sometimes the gospel is brought to a city by a preaching mission. People have been reached through hearing the gospel over the radio and through special meetings. The ways people outside the Church become Christians are many. The Spirit of God works freely through various channels. No one becomes a true Christian and no one stays a true Christian except through evangelism. And that work is never finished, for the followers of Christ must hear the gospel over and over again if they would remain Christians and grow up in the faith.

The Church is our means of Christian growth

The Church provides our best means for Christian growth. The term "means of grace" is an old one. It refers to the special practices that Christians have found most helpful to their growth as children of God. The Church is one of our choicest means of grace. In it our Christian knowledge and experience may grow. The New Testament warns Christians not to forsake the assembling of themselves together. A self-centered Christian will soon become a peculiar Christian. He will rob himself of the enrichment of the nurturing community.

The Church has always held that there are several methods through which men receive the grace of God. Among them are group worship, reading of the Bible and hearing it preached, the Lord's Supper, baptism, and prayer. Reading the Bible and preaching have always been regarded as primary means of spiritual growth. The preacher heralds forth the message of salvation. He speaks not for himself but for God, and he speaks to himself as well as to the people who hear him. His training should give him the ability to lead people into the truth.

To read or study the Bible, whether in private or in informal groups, is a means of grace that we cannot neglect. John Wesley organized his converts into small companies headed by a sponsor. He knew that the large assembly must be broken up into small, cell-like groups for spiritual growth. The best means for these groups to develop personally is for them to study the Bible, comment on its meaning, and pray informally together. Under good guidance, the individual may read—and even study—the Bible with profit. Using modern translations is exceedingly helpful. Too few churches specialize in helping their members learn to read the Bible at home. As a result they are not rooted and grounded in the Word of God.

A sacrament is an "acted" word of God. It is a visible sign and token of an invisible reality. "The highest cannot be spoken," said Goethe; "it can only be acted." When we take part in the Lord's Supper, we grow in fellowship with Christ and with other Christians. We participate in a meaningful act.

Much the same may be said of baptism, especially when baptism is practiced in worship. When persons are baptized in the presence of a congregation, this sacrament may be a means of grace to the people who remember when they came into the Church. This sacrament stimulates the mind to reflect upon its meaning. It is a corporate act of faith.

Prayer is an essential means whereby Christians grow in their experience of the grace of God and their knowledge of his love and purpose. We do not measure a Christian's life by the amount of praying he does, but by how real his prayer life is. We must be taught how to pray. This Jesus did for his disciples when they requested it. The Lord's Prayer has always been the model prayer for his disciples. It contains all the elements of true prayer. Prayer should be sincere. It should be addressed to our heavenly Father. It should include our fellow men, and it should be offered in the name or character of Jesus. Prayer should contain adoration, thanksgiving, petition for our needs, intercession for others, dedication, and praise.

There are other means of grace that the Church offers growing Christians. There is a vast treasury of devotional literature. There are biographies of great Christians. We are inspired by the lives of men like Martin Luther, John Wesley, Albert Schweitzer, Toyohiko Kagawa, and Frank C. Laubach. There are treasures of music, drama, painting, symbolry, stained glass, and music. The earth is full of sacred places—made sacred by some historic act of faith —which can be visited. A visit to these places can be a moving experience.

The Church educates us for personal maturity

The Church trains us to become mature Christians. This is an educational task. The Church is interested in every person, and it helps him grow into his fullest potential. It assists him in the solution of his emotional, intellectual, and moral problems, so that he may become whole and healthy. It gives him pastoral care when he is perplexed and guides him to resources where he may find wisdom. It provides him with an atmosphere of encouragement, friendliness, and hope. It helps young people choose the right vocations and work out an adequate philosophy of life. It helps parents build Christian homes. The Church provides people an opportunity to give to charitable causes, to support missions at home and abroad, and to join in various projects of relief and reform.

The Church provides opportunities to meet in groups to study the Christian faith. It gives qualified people an opportunity to teach church-school classes and to engage in other church work. It helps them to serve God in daily work. The Church carries on a continuous series of studies on social, economic, and international affairs to help its members understand these issues from the Christian perspective. The products of our printing presses provide a long list of informing books for the nurture of Christians.

The Church has brought many agencies into being to educate its people in the Christian way of life. They range from kindergartens in Sunday schools to colleges, universities, and theological seminaries. Most important of all is the Christian home, which is the most important school in which the teaching of the Christian faith may be most effectively done.

The Church itself must grow

The Church itself must grow. It must become mature in mind and spirit. It must not be choked by tradition, and it dare not become a servant of modern culture. There are childish churches just as there are childish Christians. Both must forget those things which are behind, and reach toward those things which are before.

If the Church is to become mature, the best young people must be recruited to be its leaders. Church members must be given more responsibility in the Church. Too many people merely go to church and hear someone else talk. All its members are a part of a church, and they will never mature if they are treated as passive infants.

As a church grows up, it will stop worrying about petty differences among denominations. Only when a church is fully mature in the great tradition of the Christian faith will it be a church that Christ can approve.

Above all, the secret of growth in the Church is in its constant exposure to the source and succor of its existence, the gospel of Jesus Christ, in the light of which it is both judged on its defects and faults and saved by self-criticism and obedient trust.

CHAPTER SIX

THE RESPONSIBLE COMMUNITY

THE CHURCH IS THE RESPONSIBLE COMMUNITY!

Through the centuries its people have taken their high calling as children of God seriously. They have not only been a source of moral renewal in personal and social life, but they have also been a persistent body of protest against injustice, immorality, unrighteousness, and inhumanity. While the primary task of the Church is to proclaim the good news of God's love in Jesus Christ, it cannot remain silent when conditions prevail which are contrary to the holy purposes of God. The Church is the creator and educator of a new conscience inspired by the law and love of God in Christ Jesus. The Church is not primarily a law school or law court but it certainly is commissioned by God to establish a new righteousness—or rightness—in history which is at once guided by the moral Law of God and motivated by the Love of God. Grace does not abolish the law; rather, it gives the sinner who continually breaks the law the will to obey the law out of gratitude for his forgiveness. Only those who repent of their guilt, and receive the grace of God are really prepared to live the life of responsibility to God and neighbor!

The responsible individual

Jesus called his disciples the salt of the earth and the light of the world. These terms have strong moral significance. Salt fights decay, and light is the enemy of darkness and infection. So Christian people are to be a preserving, revealing, and judging force in the life of society. From what we know about light, we are aware that it not only illumines the universe, but it is also a source of energy. When Jesus spoke of himself and his disciples as the light of the world, he must have had in mind the fact that they were to be the source of ethical and moral power.

The Church has not always used as much intelligence or as much courage as it should have in championing social justice and in applying the moral implications of the gospel. But it has, nevertheless, been a source of moral education. Nowhere can we see this more clearly than in non-Christian lands. A Christian in these lands is actually different from the people around him. His faith fills him with a new sense of dignity and gives him a new moral tone. The gospel not only saves men's souls; it changes the whole man; it affects his social relationships. His daily behavior improves. He manifests a new dignity in his work. He has a new feeling toward all the moral issues of life. It was this novel moral character that made the Christains of the early church such an effective witnessing power in the Greco-Roman world.

Though the Church is not primarily an ethical community, but rather a community of God's grace, it does have a moral and ethical character. It generates in its members the spirit of gratitude, of stewardship, of involvement in society, of loving concern for people. The gospel is the source of the responsible community.

70

The Church teaches the law

The Christian Church is a witness to the law of God. It maintains that God has established a law of righteousness that men dare not flout or disobey. There are some things that we cannot change. The law of God is final. It is foundational. All weights and measures in the United States are checked by the National Bureau of Standards in Washington D. C. This bureau is the final authority. There is no appeal beyond it. Just so, the law of God is the final authority in the universe.

There is a law at work in nature that we dare not disobey. This is called natural law. Let anyone play with gravity, and see what happens! There are laws to keep us healthy, and woe to the people who refuse to follow them!

Just so, say the people in the Church, there is also a law of eternal righteousness. We find this law concentrated in the Ten Commandments and in Jesus' interpretation of them in his Sermon on the Mount. It was perfectly expressed in his words and life. We must love God above all else. We must not make him into a "thing" of any kind. We must respect him and keep his name and character holy. We must honor our elders, who pass on to us the faith and wisdom of our fathers. We must respect life, purity, and property. We must not covet what belongs to another, or degrade his character. We must not lie, for this flouts truth, hurts others, and disrupts relationships with people. Jesus agreed with the ancient law but gave it a deeper personal meaning. "It is not enough," said Jesus, "for us merely to keep from doing wrong." We must do right. We must regard what is right and wrong not only in what we do, but also in what we think and

71

want and plan. Love is the highest law—love for God and for neighbor!

When the Nazis took over Holland and censored newspapers, radios, and other means of communication, people could not get accurate news from the outside world. Their minds became confused by Nazi propaganda. The air was polluted with lies. People went to church in greater numbers. In the house of God they heard the ancient law read and were often restored to their rightful minds. They lost their confusion. The law braces and clarifies. It sets minds straight by placing before them absolute standards of truth, love, and righteousness. It gives men something to stabilize personality and society by revealing the righteousness which down through the ages has not been affected by change. Robert E. Speer once commented on the clean, clear moral atmosphere which surrounds the Jesus of the gospels.

"The wages of sin is death." "Whatsoever a man soweth, that shall he also reap." "And every one that heareth these sayings of mine, and doeth them not, shall be likened unto a foolish man, which built his house upon the sand." "Ye cannot serve God and mammon." Who can quarrel with these absolutes! Such Bible verses as these declare that people and nations who disobey God's law are under judgment. Those who try to break the law will be broken by it. To defy Jesus Christ and build the house of life on another foundation is sheer folly.

The Church produces responsible citizens

Being a Christian is not merely a matter of believing in a creed, or enjoying a worship service, or delighting in the "ideas" of the Christian faith. Being a Christian includes all these and more. The deep inner self must be brought into obedience to Jesus Christ as Lord and Savior. When this happens, life is under "new management." It belongs to Christ who claims it utterly by his love.

Christians who confess Christ as Lord use their freedom in a responsible way. They are moved by the power of love. They are not controlled from without but from within. A new law is written in their hearts; that law is a personal relation to the living Christ. Christians acknowledge that they are stewards of the grace of God in Christ. They regard the good earth and its fruits, life and all that sustains it, as gifts of God. They own all things, yet they own nothing, for they are owned by God. They live in their Father's world. We might call them "moneyless magnates." As stewards their lives are offered to, and glorify or manifest, God. They are engaged in full-time Christian service. The whole of life is a ministry, a vocation engaged in the service of God. All Christians are ministers of God, whether they serve in factory, home, field, schoolroom, office, or church.

Christians are world citizens. They are involved in the humanity for which Christ lived, died, and rose again. They are not of the world, but are in the world and for the world. They are sensitive to the injustices among races and social classes. They protest against the intolerable conditions under which men have to live and work. They do a good day's work, and they seek to promote the common welfare of all who work. They use their vocations for the glory of God and the good of men. In short, as Christian citizens they set themselves against everything that flouts the will of Christ and degrades man. They work for social conditions that are favorable to the purpose of God for all men. They bring about a better society. The

Church is the school that leads men into the deep significance and wide ramifications of the new life in Christ.
Such a life is anything but passive. Rather it is active and
aggressive in its concern to make Jesus Christ lord in every
area of life and in every part of the world. The Christian's
life is one of creative goodness, inspired not by legal com-
pulsion but by free gratitude generated by the forgiving
grace of God.

The Church makes the Christian conscience

The Church performs an educational task of creating
the Christian conscience. The prophetic mission of the
Church is to throw the light of divine truth on every as-
pect of life. The Church is commissioned to diagnose the
evils in the world, to call men to repentance, and to con-
front them with the decisive claims of God upon their
lives.

The Church expresses the Christian conscience through
its ministers, its agencies, its publications, its schools, and
its people. Many groups of Christians who are keenly aware
of the Church's responsibility to and for society are carry-
ing on studies and conversations with a view to bringing
this Christian conscience to bear upon practices that are
not Christian. These groups have issued valuable pamph-
lets and books on such subjects as war, colonialism, the
race problem, the use of atom and hydrogen bombs, na-
tionalism, and communism. They write from the Christian
viewpoint.

Denominational bodies and church councils draft official statements on issues of unusual significance; these
statements are given wide publicity. Some people disap-
prove of such pronouncements, and we must agree they
do not seem to bring about large results. They represent,

however, the creative study of some of our best Christian minds. They help to crystallize the thought of Christian people, and they serve as guides for further study and action on social issues. They witness to the Christian perspective.

Most denominations and church councils have committees on social education and action. The National Council of Churches and the World Council of Churches have large and influential committees that constantly study the relation of the Christian faith to social and international issues. They conduct conferences, publish studies, and often send delegations of able leaders to present the Christian viewpoint to Congress, to the President, and to the United Nations.

To cite one example: A number of years ago the National Council of Churches formed twelve guiding principles for international affairs:

1. WE BELIEVE that moral law, no less than physical law, undergirds our world. There is a moral order which is fundamental and eternal, and which is relevant to the corporate life of men and the ordering of human society. . . .

2. WE BELIEVE that the sickness and suffering which afflict our present society are proof of indifference to, as well as direct violation of, the moral law. All share in responsibility for the present evils. . . .

3. WE BELIEVE that it is contrary to the moral order that nations in their dealings with one another should be motivated by a spirit of revenge and retaliation. . . .

4. WE BELIEVE that the principle of cooperation and

75

mutual concern, implicit in the moral order and essential to a just and durable peace, calls for a true community of nations. The interdependent life of nations must be ordered by agencies having the duty and the power to promote and safeguard the general welfare of all people. . . .

5. WE BELIEVE that economic security is no less essential than political security to a just and durable peace. Such security nationally and internationally involves among other things the use of material resources and the tools of production to raise the general standard of living. . . .

6. WE BELIEVE that international machinery is required to facilitate the easing of such economic and political tensions as are inevitably recurrent in a world which is living and therefore changing. . . .

7. WE BELIEVE that the government which derives its just powers from the consent of the governed is the truest expression of the rights and dignity of man. This requires that we seek autonomy for all subject and colonial peoples. . . .

8. WE BELIEVE that military establishments should be internationally controlled and be made subject to law under the community of nations. . . .

9. WE BELIEVE that the right of all men to pursue work of their own choosing and to enjoy security from want and oppression is not limited by race, color or creed. . . .

10. WE BELIEVE that, in bringing international relations into conformity with the moral law, a very heavy responsibility devolves upon the United States. . . .

11. WE BELIEVE that, as Christian citizens, we must seek to translate our beliefs into practical realities and to create a public opinion which will insure that the United States shall play its full and essential part in the creation of a moral way of international living. . . .

12. WE BELIEVE that a supreme responsibility rests with the Church. The Church, being a creation of God in Jesus Christ, is called to proclaim to all men everywhere the way of life. Moreover, the Church which is now in reality a world community, may be used of God to develop His spirit of righteousness and love in every race and nation and thus to make possible a just and durable peace. . . .

While these statements regarding a just and durable peace have been amplified and amended since, they indicate the thrust of the Christian conscience on social affairs.

The Church speaks on social issues

At the Amsterdam Assembly of the World Council of Churches the church leaders spoke on the disorders in society and in the world. Attention was directed to two dangers in our modern world, the use of technical machinery, and concentrated power. It declared that concentrated power tends to bring about greed, pride, and cruelty, and to take responsibility away from the individual person. Totalitarian power robs man of his freedom and destroys his personality. Technical machinery does away with drudgery, but it also creates mass population centers, makes for greater destruction in war, and undermines the family, the neighborhood, and the use of crafts in industry. People are no longer closely bound together. Technical machinery also tends to waste God's gifts of natural resources. God created us to be free, responsible to him and to our neighbors. When any government keeps men from acting in a responsible way, this is a denial of what God intends for them. Man must not be made a mere means for political and social ends. Man is not made for the state but the state for man. Man is not made for production but production is made for man. A responsible society will let men be free to control, criticize, and change their government. In it power will be made responsible to law and tradition, and will be widely shared among the people in the society. The Church condemns anything that limits its freedom to witness for its Lord and his plans for men. It condemns any attempt to take away our freedom to obey God and act as our conscience tells us to act. A responsible society will give us the right to share in shaping our world.

In regard to the international situation the church leaders at Amsterdam stated that the world is in God's hands, that his purpose may be thwarted for a while but cannot finally fail. Christian people must not despair, nor surrender to the fascinating belief that power offers the solution to man's troubles. These leaders declared that war is against the will of God. Even those who thought that defensive war sometimes becomes a duty once conflict breaks out, were aware of the injustice of mass destruction in modern warfare. We are finding it more and more difficult to call any war just.

The Church must attack the causes of war and promote peaceful change through the pursuit of justice. This means it must uphold the integrity of the pledged word. It must resist imperial power. It must work to reduce arms. It must keep people from indifference and despair when they are faced with the futility of war. If men want peace, they must attack the causes of conflict. Conflict develops when men divide into opposing groups, when nations attack other nations for their own gain, and when totalitarian systems compete with one another. Also they must acknowledge the rule of law. They must recognize its authority, establish it in the way of life, and build our institutions around it. The churches have an important part in laying the foundations of moral conviction without which any system will break down.

The church leaders at Amsterdam affirmed that "all men are equal in the sight of God and that the rights of men derive directly from their status as the children of God." No one state should presume that it can grant or deny these rights. Both men and states must remember there are no rights without duties.

Church leaders have taken a firm stand against groups who violate human rights, as well as those who discriminate against races, religions, or cultures. They have protested against countries that expel minority groups. They have upheld freedom of speech, of expression, of association, and of assembly. They have upheld the rights of the family. They have opposed forced arrest and forced segregation and have supported a fuller realization of man's freedom through laws. They have defended the dignity and the freedom of men.

The Amsterdam Assembly received and commended to the churches a statement on religious liberty that said: "(1) every person has the right to determine his own faith and creed. . . . (2) every person has the right to express his religious beliefs in worship, teaching, and practice. . . . (3) every person has the right to associate with others and to organise with them for religious purposes. . . . (4)

79

every religious organisation . . . has the right to determine its policies and practices for the accomplishment of its chosen purposes."

What was discussed and crystallized at Amsterdam was reiterated and amplified at the Evanston Assembly. New situations had arisen to make new applications of the Christian conscience necessary. The report said:

"Responsible society" is not an alternative social or political system, but a criterion by which we judge all existing social orders and at the same time a standard to guide us in the specific choices we have to make. Christians are called to live responsibly, to live in response to God's act of redemption in Christ, in any society, even within the most unfavourable social structures.

A reading of the reports of the Amsterdam and Evanston Assemblies, as well as the statements and pronouncements of the National Council of Churches and the assemblies and conferences of denominational bodies will indicate the penetrating and persistent way in which the Church is seeking to fulfill its ethical mission in the world.

The Church as a responsible community

The Church cannot attack the injustices in the world unless it first admits that many of them are found in its own household. It is the Church's business to renew its life, to overcome national, social, economic, and racial barriers within itself, and to practice a new obedience to Jesus Christ as Lord. Sometimes the Church has contributed to the very ills that trouble people outside the Church. Sometimes, as was said at Amsterdam, the Church has lent its approval to the privileges of dominant classes, and certain racial and political groups. Sometimes it has stressed its spiritual life to the neglect of its responsibility to society. The Church will be more effective in society if it will be genuinely Christian in its fellowship, and if it will teach and inspire its members to live and work in the world in the spirit of responsibility.

CHAPTER SEVEN

THE DIVINE-HUMAN FELLOWSHIP

THE CHURCH IS THE DIVINE-HUMAN FELLOWSHIP!
The world is full of fellowships. What is the difference between the Church and other fellowships? The Church does some things that all institutions and organizations do, and yet it is more than just an organization or an institution. Fundamentally, the Church is not an organization but a fellowship of persons. It is a fellowship that has about it a certain spirit and character.

The nature of Christian fellowship

The early Christians of New Testament days had a real sense of organic unity. The Christians of Jersualem "were of one heart and of one soul: neither said any of them that aught of the things which he possessed was his own; but they had all things common." The Greek word for this common life is *koinonia*. It means "having things in common."

Jesus sought early to impress on his followers how their fellowship was different from other fellowships. As the disciples quarreled among themselves as to who was the greatest, he washed their feet. In this way he sought to teach them the fellowship of humility and service. As he, their Lord and Master, had served them, so they ought to love and serve one another. When he instituted the sacrament of the Lord's Supper, he hoped to teach them this same lesson, only in a more dramatic, unforgettable, and intimate way.

This sense of fellowship develops all through the New Testament. Starting with Jesus and the Twelve it takes on more meaningfulness through the Acts of the Apostles and the epistles. The New Testament speaks of the Church as the brotherhood, the household of God, the household of faith, and a colony of heaven. It has been maintained that there are more than eighty terms used by writers in the New Testament to describe the Church. We have mentioned only a few of these terms. This bond between Christians and Jesus Christ is such that even eighty terms are not sufficient to adequately designate the nature of the Christian fellowship. No one of them should be used exclusively. Christians are referred to as salt, light, God's plantation, God's harvest, the vineyard, the vine and the branches, lights, olive tree, the bridal party, the bride of Christ, the holy city, servants, freemen, a royal priesthood, a holy nation, called, chosen, stewards, saints, believers, faithful, God's temple, the flock, the elect exiles of the dispersion, and many other terms.

A new kind of togetherness was felt by the people who joined the Christian community. Jews and Gentiles, men and women, were recipients of God's grace and sharers in the life and work of Christ. Slaves and freemen were joined together in a new way as equals. The middle wall of partition between people and groups was broken down in Christ. The accidents of race and nationality were transcended; in Christ, all these differences were overcome by the new man in Christ. For a person to become a member in the Church depended solely upon his relationship to the one head of the Church. All members were one in Christ. As all men were one in Adam, so they are now united in Christ. "As in Adam all die, even so in Christ shall all be made alive." They shared their joys and sorrows, and even their goods. They cared for one another and sought in love to help the weak and to correct graciously those who needed it.

A common meal was the high point of their worship, a ceremony that pointed them back to Christ's sacrificial love that had brought their fellowship into being. It also pointed forward to the time when they would share in the banquet of the fulfilled kingdom of God. This fellowship was a joyous one, yet it filled Christians with the urge to hurry and tell the gospel of the new age to all men. The people of the Church felt that they were part of this new age. They lived in anticipation of the Kingdom, as they already shared its actual power in their lives.

The Church is a suprafellowship

The fellowship of the Church has some characteristics that we do not find elsewhere. At the Oxford Conference on Life and Work in 1937 it was said that the Gospel upon which the Church is founded claims the "whole man, spirit, mind, and body, and every human institution for the service of God." The Gospel is for every man. It knows no boundaries of race, nation, class, age, or sex. The Church knows only persons, created in the image of God, judged by the law of God, and redeemed by the grace of God. It knows that there are differences among people, but it does not regard these differences as the most important thing about them.

The Church is a supraclass fellowship—that is, a fellowship that is above class distinctions. It is a great leveler. It does not level all men *down* to a low standard, but *up* to a higher one. A Christian is a member of a one-class community. Citizenship in this community goes beyond any differences among its members. The Church is concerned about men as children of God. And because the Church is concerned about justice and the dignity and development of all men in freedom, it is interested in raising all men to a higher level of thought and life. The Church cannot tolerate social distinctions that exalt some and degrade others. Nor can it stand by when people act irresponsibly, whether they are among the privileged few or among the masses.

The Church is also a supraracial fellowship—that is, a fellowship that is above race distinctions. It includes men of every race. These races are not equally developed and are not the same in temperament or character, but God created them all, and each has its place in his purpose. All races are of equal worth to God. The Church that is true to the gospel cannot tolerate segregation and racial discrimination. Indeed, its task is more than that of protest; it must encourage conditions which are conducive to the fullest development of all races.

The Church is also a supranational fellowship. It is a fellowship that transcends patriotism. Christians in the different nations have more in common with one another than they have with their non-Christian fellow citizens. The Church instills in them a loyalty to God that is above and beyond their loyalty to men. This high loyalty makes good citizens, since it gives them a high sense of responsibility toward the nation of which they are citizens. Christians desire only the best for their nations under God. They are their nation's best citizens. During World War II the churches kept alive a bond of union among Christians. Few prayers of hatred were uttered in them. This world-wide unity among Christians is a strong force for the growth of world unity. The Church is the world-wide community in which a basic universal confidence is at work—a confidence that produces a fellowship of understanding among all men.

The Church is also a supratemporal fellowship. It is a fellowship that cannot be limited by time. D. R. Davies has suggested that the Church fulfills its mission in eternity while all other societies fulfill their missions in time. The Church sees beyond the span of time and history. It calls people to become citizens of the eternal City of God. It sees all events from the perspective of God's all-embracing purpose. It is a constant reminder to the nations of the context of God's eternal purpose, lest they loose "wild tongues" that do not hold God in awe.

The Church is a fellowship of forgiveness and reconciliation

In 1925, after World War I, an ecumenical gathering of churches was held in Stockholm, Sweden. The late Archbishop Söderblom, of the Swedish Church, spoke with deep feeling as he addressed the delegates from the nations that had been at war. The bitterness caused by that conflict had not yet disappeared. Many of the delegates remembered the losses their countries had sustained, the terrible things that had been said on both sides, and the atrocities that had been committed. But in this church gathering they joined in the spirit of Christ. In their allegiance to him they found a common unity. The sessions of that great gathering were marked by a spirit of brotherhood.

When the assembly of the World Council of Churches met in Amsterdam in 1948, after World War II, it issued some remarkable statements on this truth. Section I of the report reads:

God has given to His people in Jesus Christ a unity which is His creation and not our achievement. We praise and thank Him for a mighty work of His Holy Spirit, by which we have been drawn together to discover that, notwithstanding our divisions, we are one in Jesus Christ.
. . . We come from Christian churches which have for long misunderstood, ignored and misrepresented one another;
. . . we are all sinful men and we are heirs to the sins of our fathers. We do not deserve the blessing which God has given us.

.   .   .   .

It is in the light of that unity that we face our deepest difference, still loving one another in Christ and walking by faith in Him alone. . . . It exists among many other differences of emphasis within Christendom.

The report continues:

We have found God, in His mercy, penetrating the barriers of our fundamental division and enabling us to speak, in the common language of the divine revelation witnessed to us in the Scriptures. . . . Wherever we find ourselves thus speaking together of our unity, we also find ourselves faced by some stubborn problems. In dealing with them, we discover disagreements . . . and, beneath those disagreements, we find again an agreement in a unity which drew us together and will not let us go.

The church leaders at the Assembly confessed that pride, self-will, and the lack of love have played and still play a part in making and keeping divisions in the Church. The evils of the world have deeply penetrated the churches: these evils have resulted in worldly standards of success, class division, economic rivalry, and worldliness among church members. Even though some churches do not differ in their theology, their language, or their forms of worship, they are separated by race and color, a scandal in the body of Christ.

Churches have often been so occupied with their own affairs that they have forgotten to give their love and service to others. Often the officers in a church have so dominated it that the members of the church could not have real Christian fellowship together.

Thus did the churches at Amsterdam express themselves. Out of their sense of sinfulness came a real willingness to be reconciled to one another and to live together in the spirit of forgiveness. And what they affirmed at Amsterdam, they reaffirmed with greater vigor and clearer understanding at Evanston.

If the Church is to be what God intended it to be and what Christ seeks to make it, it must fulfill its high calling by seeking through repentance to reconcile different groups, such as young people and adults, men and women, the wise and the ignorant, Chinese and Americans, Russians and Indians, the rich and the poor, the East and the West. In the Church, people of the world can and do become brothers through Christ, who breaks down the middle wall of partition and brings peace through the new man he creates. A church filled with the spirit of repentance and faith can generate and propagate an atmosphere of self-criticism and hopeful confidence, and thus be a light in a dark world.

The Church is the fellowship of the new order

The Church is a community of promise and hope. It points to a redeemed world. It is our assurance that God will save his people and that his kingdom will be fully realized some day. Even now men from all nations and races and tribes of the earth are gathering into the Church. They are forming the abiding and increasing sign and evidence of the coming kingdom of God.

The Church is the frontier of the Kingdom, the point at which God's rule invades the world. It is the community in which God's new order is already at work. Because it must protest against the false nature of life in the world and live in a society of people who do not obey God's rule, like Jesus, the Church is a pilgrim on the earth. It lives a broken life. It is the world's best friend and finest hope; yet the world often hates and despises it. Being a member of the Church is not easy, because it means being a member of a community of people who are constantly protesting against a sinful world, constantly maladjusted to a world that is not real, and constantly agonizing for the world of God's intention.

The Church achieves fellowship

If the Church would fulfill its high calling, it will seek to achieve fellowship. The people employed by the Church are members of the fellowship, and we cannot treat them in a mere businesslike way.

Ministers need to think carefully about their relationships with their music and religious-education directors, with their associates, with their office staff, and with the other employees in the church. The relationship among ministers in different churches and in church councils must also be brought to the bar of Christ's judgment.

Large churches need to discover ways for their members to get acquainted with one another, to associate in small groups, and to know the meaning of community.

Churches that are made up of a single social class need to seek ways to represent all the classes of humanity in their community lest they become exclusive social clubs and fail to be the Christian community. Progress in this respect is being made in many parts of the world Church. Creative experiments are in evidence.

Fellowship must also be achieved in Christian families. The home is also in the Church and it is perhaps the most significant social unit. Churches can do much to educate young people for marriage and to help marriages succeed through proper counseling and other wise assistance. Marriage is a high form of Christian fellowship, and the Christian home is the finest type of Christian community possible. Our churches ought to be especially concerned that marriages take place between persons who understand the meaning of the mutual priesthood of believers, so that the Church may be found in the homes of the parish and founded upon such homes.

A church that is seeking to achieve unity in its families and in itself will also be a church that awakens a spirit of unity in its community. It will look on the neighborhood in which it works as its parish. It will seek to radiate out into it the spirit of reconciliation. Not only will such a church be interested in the community, it will be at the center of the community. It will never isolate itself in the spirit of self-protection; rather, as the body of Christ, it will give itself for the life of the community. The community is the latent or potential church, and as such the local congregation is the servant of the community.

The problem of human unity

One of the most pressing problems of our time is, How can men live together in unity? Many new attempts to establish a better social order are in evidence everywhere. Fascism and communism are efforts to achieve community. They are social "isms," each seeking to help people to live together in unity. Many new attempts to establish a better social order are in evidence everywhere. These social "isms" have stabbed the Church awake to reconsider what Christian fellowship is like and to sense its responsibility for community in a badly divided world. W. A. Visser 't Hooft, the general secretary of the World Council of Churches, writes in *The Christian Century*:

Not only is the Church a community of people who know about God's new order and accept it, it is at the same time the nucleus of the new order, the channel through which it enters the world, the shock troops by which it is prepared. It is the new people of the future in a world held in chains by the past. The Church is therefore not merely called to announce the new order of God; it is called to represent, *to be* that new order. It is called *to be* the new lump, the salt of the earth.

The Church is called on, especially in times like these, to witness to the things that make for a just and true order, for freedom and unity.

A fellowship of this kind is what God intends for all men, especially at a time when the whole world needs and seeks a new spirit of unity. The cry for social justice is not a cry for bread so much as it is a demand for people and nations to find meaning for their lives. Millions of people have lost their sense of belonging to one another. They feel desperately lonely and forsaken. They have no neighbors. To submit to the organizational life is the death of personal life; to continue in individual license is slavery of the worst kind. It is the Church's major task to achieve Christian fellowship for its own sake and for the sake of the world. Thus it will make its greatest contribution. Perhaps our greatest barrier in achieving fellowship in the world is an unfaithful Church.

This situation is being brought home to the churches in penetrating ways. It is rather trite to repeat the statement of the late Archbishop Temple that the emergence of the world reality of the Church is the great new fact of our time. But it is true! The Church is called to be the spearhead of God's new humanity and of man's new social home by the imperious demand of all men for fellowship, and its nature and mission according to the charter of its faith in the Scriptures, and particularly in the God-Man, Jesus Christ, the light and Lord of the world!

CHAPTER EIGHT

THE BEARER OF THE CHRISTIAN TRADITION

THE CHURCH IS THE BEARER OF THE CHRISTIAN TRADITION!

The word "tradition" means that which is carried over from one generation to the next. It represents the accumulation and crystallization of the past. Everyone at birth enters that which already exists. The world is full of traditions. We inherit our traditions from the generations that went before us, we do not create them. We could not live without them. We receive institutions, ideas, attitudes, customs, languages, religions, and a great many other things.

A nation has its traditions. "America" and "The Star-Spangled Banner" are a part of our American national heritage. So are our customs, our proverbs, our festivals, and the ways we dress. So are the men who founded our country and other great men who have loved it in the past and added to the wealth of its life. Education to a large extent is bringing our children into an appreciation of the past, so that they will understand it, enter into it, accept it as their own, criticize and correct its faults, and contribute to our country's future.

The Church preserves and presents us with the great tradition that embodies and carries the highest values men have ever known. The Church has handed down from generation to generation a vast amount of priceless tradition in the form of literature, symbolism, doctrines, stories, hymns, liturgies, paintings, and monuments. Christians in the early Church had no traditions, except those of the Old Testament. They repeated the stories of Jesus' life, death, and resurrection, by word of mouth. Gradually, they and their successors built up traditions, which have been enriched from generation to generation. Much of it is preserved in literature and creed and liturgy and institution. It is surprising to note how much of our Christianity is inherited from the past, and how much of what we think and do is custom and habit. We may be grateful that so much that is valuable in the past has been kept alive to inspire and guide men to create greater traditions for the people who come after them.

The reality of Christian tradition

It is a thrilling and enlightening experience to visit another country. It is like entering another world. People speak a language different from our own. They eat strange foods prepared in ways which are not familiar to us. Their habit of dress is unusual. Their social customs are not like those to which we are accustomed. But even stranger to us than these outward differences are the differences in their traditions. The people of these foreign lands have a different background from ours. They, too, have their national heroes, their patron saints, their sacred shrines, their folklore, their customary ways of thinking, their group spirit, and their national celebrations. They are proud of their ancestors. Indeed, in some places they worship them. They are united through symbols, stories, heroes, soil, group spirit, and a strange feeling of kinship with their ancestors. If we simply pay a hurried visit to a country, we never enter fully into the life of its people. If we would know another country, we must know the spirit and background of its people. The people of every country have their traditions which are taught their young people through discipline, education, and example.

Few people think of the Church as having such a tradition. Yet down through the past two thousand years Christian people have been expressing, preserving, and interpreting the finest and richest traditions of their faith. They have passed on to those who followed them meaningful customs, beliefs, stories, literature, art, history, and music. Perhaps these are the best bequests the generations have inherited. Sometimes these priceless treasures have been preserved at the cost of life itself. We marvel that they have been preserved and even enriched during the centuries through life and death, the rise and fall of nations, the carelessness and sinfulness of the people, and the hostility of enemies.

The Church is a "holy nation." Like a nation it, too, has its history, which is filled with varied lore. To know the Christian tradition we must accept it humbly. We must be willing to do whatever is necessary to become participating and intelligent members in this historic community. We must learn the language of the Church. We must want to do more than just sit in a pew once in a while. The pity is that many people, even church members, know so little of the story of the Church and what the long history and thrilling tradition of the Church are really like. Christians are heirs of the grace of

God in Christ and the effects of this grace in thought, beauty, and action upon the generations affected by it. By neglecting this birthright, they rob themselves of a sense of belonging to a great heritage. Perhaps no one has ever properly helped them to know their Christian inheritance. An undiscovered country of great value lies waiting for the Christian who would adventure into it.

The tradition of thought

To realize how Christ has influenced men's thoughts, all one needs to do is enter a modern library and look through the stacks. Book after book will indicate the power of Jesus Christ to make men think about God and the highest things in life.

Someone has called Jesus the "Lord of thought." He does not teach us science, or modern history, or political and economic theories. But his message of truth is certainly relevant to their basic issues. The scientist deals with God's creation, but the uses to which scientists put this creation is related to the truth about God and man. History is the stage upon which men work out their salvation or damnation; history must meet the truth. Political and economic systems cannot avoid God's truth about people, nations, and races.

The Church is a fellowship of people in whom the mind of Christ is at work to make men free in the truth. This mind has perhaps been the strongest influence on men's thoughts that history has ever known. The process of creating the Christian mind has been going on for hundreds of years and it has involved millions of people. And out of it has come a marvelous deposit of Christian thinking.

In every age Christians have thought and thought

96

about their faith as they tried to interpret
selves and their generation, to crystallize it
containers and transmit it to their children
oncoming generations.

Think of the great creeds of the Church, s
Nicene Creed, the Apostles' Creed, the A
Creed, the catechisms, and other majestic stat
faith. These are crystallized forms of Christian
often forged in the fiery furnaces of controversy
secution when Christians had to know clearly w
believed. Creeds were not made in a day. They
product of years of intellectual development and s
and of many minds influenced by the gospel. Cr
not have the authority that the Bible has, but th
precious deposits of thought. They are the great
of the Christian mind. They light up our confused
with the truths that our fellow Christians of other
lived by, and often died for.

But there is more to Christian thought than
creeds. Christians think about everything from Go
man, from the beginning of history to the fulfilling
God's plan for the world. They make a special study
theology, which is knowledge about God. Theol
deals with the meaning of life, its problems and its
vation, in the light of the Word of God. These are
sues that concern every man. Theology seeks to unde
stand and to interpret God's will to men. One of th
most urgent tasks for Christians is to love God with
the mind and the heart and to make clear to others the
saving power of his truth.

Throughout its long history, the Church has gathered
together a storehouse of wisdom that is based on the
Word of God. The Church's task is to interpret this wis-

dom so that men's minds may be filled with the light of truth. Today, there is no greater need than the need to think clearly.

We live in an age of serious and active thought. New conditions demand new ideas. Everywhere, men are forced to think seriously about the ultimate issues. Christians are rethinking the meaning of their faith as they are faced with bewildering situations and open hostility. We must think straight if our minds are to be saved from the darkness of error, the confusion of propaganda, and the disintegration of a mind set on anything less than the highest. If we are not certain in our minds about what life means, we become anxious and fearful. What we believe is desperately important.

Throughout the history of the Christian Church the difficult periods have become the creative periods of Christian thought. It was in those days that theology became more than a playground for intellectuals. It became a field in which people thought clearly and acted on their high convictions. Theology became a necessity in people's lives. It was something by which to live. Theology is again coming into its own as the queen of the sciences, as the marching orders of Christianity, and as the highest and best wisdom of life. It is the crucial concern of every man.

The tradition of art

Christians have always used symbols to express their faith, to stimulate their memory, and to fix their thoughts on holy things. To represent the Church they used an ark, or ship. This was the symbol of the ark of salvation, the refuge of the redeemed sailing on the stormy sea of life. We call the long body of a large church the nave, which is derived from the Latin word *navis*, meaning "ship."

The early Christians left us many samples of their art. We find traces of their symbols in the Roman catacombs. The figure of a fish, for instance, which was a symbol for Christ. Each letter of the Greek word for fish is the first letter of a word they used to express their faith—Jesus Christ, Son of God, Savior. The art and symbolism of the early church reveal a simplicity and power that is typical of a fighting faith.

The butterfly is a symbol of the Resurrection because it comes to life out of what seems to be a dead cocoon. The peacock is a symbol of new, or eternal life because its feathers take on a more glorious color at molting time. The circle symbolizes eternity or God. Three circles intertwined symbolize the Trinity. The Trinity is also represented by a triangle, by a figure made up of two triangles put together to form a star, by a shamrock, by a fleur-de-lis (a flower very much like the iris), and by a trefoil. A hand thrust downward symbolizes the hand of God. A lamb lying on a book closed with seven seals is a symbol of the Lamb of God, who alone is worthy to open the story of history. A candle stands for Christ, who is the light of the world. A descending dove symbolizes the Holy Spirit coming down from God. The candelabra with seven branches, or the flame with seven tongues, stands for the seven gifts of the Holy Spirit—power, riches, wisdom, strength, honor, glory, and blessing. There is a symbol for each of the twelve disciples except Judas. Each of these symbols shows us what the disciple was like in his character and his work.

In fact, we could use symbols to tell the whole story of redemption as we have it in the Bible. The Church

I BELIEVE IN THE CHURCH

is a treasure house of symbols that Christians have worked out and that bear the sanction and authority of centuries of experience. These symbols make our faith more real to us and help us to concentrate in worship. In Protestant churches no use is made of human figures in worship and teaching. We do not feel that human figures can be used to represent the eternal things of God. We use symbols instead.

Christianity is highly dramatic. The story of Christianity as we find it in the Bible is a great drama in two parts, opening with a prologue and closing with an epilogue. Every service of worship in a church ought to partake of the beauty and symmetry of that great drama of redemption. It should be an act that brings to mind the greatest story ever told. It is also a part of the drama of the Church year. The Church year starts with Advent, or the preparation of the stage for the coming of Christ. It goes on through the birth and ministry and passion and death of Jesus Christ, to his resurrection and ascension. It continues through the coming of the Holy Spirit, the birth of the Church and of Christian experience, the launching of the new community, and on to the coming of God's kingdom, when God's plan for the world will finally be fulfilled.

The Church has inspired some of the noblest music ever written. The music of the Passion has perhaps the deepest meaning of all music ever composed. Oratorios, cantatas, symphonies, and even dramatic operas are all a living part of the tradition of the Church. And not the least among the prized possessions of the Church is the hymnbook, that treasury of the songs of the faithful, in which words and music are finely blended to produce one of the most unusual books men have ever

100

compiled. To open a hymnbook is to enter the community of sacred song that has been singing through the centuries. The whole Christian faith is found in the hymnbook.

The Christian faith has produced its own literature. Some of our greatest classics were inspired by religion— John Bunyan's *Pilgrim's Progress,* Augustine's *Confessions,* John Wesley's *Journals,* and Martin Luther's *Freedom of the Christian Man.* We have but to think of these books to appreciate the world of great literature that has been born in and preserved by the Church. Although we do not think of them as Christian classics, many of the greatest books in our literature have been inspired by the gospel story, by the lives of Christian heroes, or by the struggles of the Church against its enemies. Who can measure the influence of the gospel story on Shakespeare, Carlyle, Dickens, Tennyson, Lowell, Emerson, Goethe, Dostoevski, T. S. Eliot, and others?

This vast inheritance is known by all too few. And because so few people know about it, the lives of most Christians are starved and dwarfed. They are cut off from the dowry that is theirs by right, and they are the poorer for it.

The tradition of life

To enter the life of the Church is to enter a relationship with all the Christians who have ever lived and who are alive now. When you marry, you marry one person. But you also become a member of a new family. When you join the fellowship of the Church, you become a member of the family of Christians of all times. And what people these Christians have been! And what a

101

history the Christian community has had! True, some people who call themselves Christians have given a bad name to the Church and to Christ. But most Christians in the history of the Church have given it a priceless heritage. Every church, in imagination, is a kind of spiritual Westminster Abbey in which we are surrounded with a great cloud of venerable witnesses.

To join the Church is to belong to the same community that Paul, Augustine, Luther, Calvin, Wesley, Fox, and Williams belonged to! These ancients can inspire us today. The author of the Epistle to the Hebrews mentioned a long list of Biblical heroes to encourage his despairing readers. He bade them to take a look at this marvelous company of men and women lest they surrender too easily in their trials and fail to press on in the spirit of the martyrs. By faith, he said, these men "gained a good report." By faith they endured suffering and temptation and imprisonment.

Wherefore seeing we also are compassed about with so great a cloud of witnesses, let us lay aside every weight, and the sin which doth so easily beset us, and let us run with patience the race that is set before us, Looking unto Jesus the author and finisher of our faith; who for the joy that was set before him endured the cross, despising the shame, and is set down at the right hand of the throne of God.

And he bids his readers consider Jesus, his endurance in crucifixion and in face of "contradiction of sinners" lest they be weary and faint in their minds.

We must remember, too, that all the brave Christians did not live in the past. We have martyrs in our own age—believers who have been persecuted for their faith and have lost their lives defending it. Many of these martyrs are little known, or even unknown to us.

Throughout its history, the Church has passed through many great crises. It has been faced with hostile governments. In some places angry men have threatened to do away with it entirely, even in our time. But, in spite of dungeon, fire, and sword, the faith of the fathers is living still. Indeed, Bishop Berggrav was quite right when he said, "When truth becomes holy, it makes martyrs." The blood of the martyrs is the seed of the Church.

The Church has sent missionaries to the ends of the earth. We think of Morrison, Judson, Nommensen, Grenfell, Carey, Moffatt, Livingstone, and hundreds of others. The Church has inspired popular education, social reform, equality among men, temperance, the Christian family, and more worthy causes than we could number. The tradition of the Church includes a great many elements, since the Church has touched life at every point. It would be interesting to trace the traditions of the Church in its dealings with the physically and mentally ill. The contest of the Church with kings and governments which have tried to run the Church or bend it to their ends is a thrilling one, indeed. But, perhaps one of the most interesting traditions of the Church has to do with the missionary enterprise at home and abroad.

Take a quick glance at the table of contents of some textbooks on the history of the Church, such as Lars Qualben's *History of the Christian Church,* Henry Rowe's *History of the Christian People,* William A. Gifford's *The Story of the Faith,* or Williston Walker's *History of the Christian Church.* You will see the long, varied, interesting, and rich record of the Church. It has developed from a small group of Christians in a pagan world into a world-wide community. It has expanded through the efforts of missionaries to nearly every country on earth. It has engaged in long and sometimes bitter controversies over matters of faith and order and practice. These experiences have left a rich deposit of Christian thought and life. We rob ourselves of great resources for guidance and courage in our living when we ignore or neglect this legacy.

Paul could say, "All things are yours; whether Paul, or Apollos, or Cephas." To this list we add the record of twenty centuries in which God's Word and Spirit have been at work in and through Christians and the Christian community. We are not the first Christians. We are the benefactors of their labors. We can learn much from those who have gone before us.

Past tradition and present living

Today, the Church faces two major problems among others. The younger churches are in desperate need of more tradition to give them balance and maturity in dealing with rapid social change in a time when they are becoming independent of foreign mission control. Without the guidance of tradition and without relatedness to the old and the traditional, they often fly off in all sectarian directions. In South Africa, for instance, the Christian movement among the natives has developed into nearly fifteen hundred groups! Yet, great patience must be exercised toward these new Christians. Their situation is like that of the Corinthian Church in Paul's day. This Church did not lack the dynamics of the Spirit; what it needed was the temperance of the more excellent way. Younger churches should not be dominated by the older churches which would dampen their enthusiasm; they should be befriended through a necessary period of adolescent growth involving storm and stress into the balanced life of age. Even so, the younger churches possess a dynamic life of youth which is the envy of the older churches. Tradition has its place; yet every church, like every Christian, has to make its own tradition, guided to be sure by the wisdom of the fathers.

On the other hand, the older churches are weighed down by traditions. Their traditions have become their grave clothes, making them immobile and irrelevant to their times. Older churches find it difficult if not impossible to be born again. Their traditions have become so dominant as to incapacitate them to meet the dynamic revolutionary spirit of the age. Cathedrals may be the products of a vital faith of the past, but they may become the tombs of the present generation. Valuable and venerable as tradition is, it cannot become the faith of the present generation of Christians without living faith.

While we can learn much from other Christians, both living and dead, we cannot rely on them for our own faith. Each of us must become a Christian by himself. We can learn from history, but we must make history of our own. The Word and the Spirit have made Christian history and heritage. The Word and the Spirit still seek to make them.

NOTES

Page	Line	
79	29	*The First Assembly of the World Council of Churches,* ed. W. A. Visser't Hooft (New York: Harper and Bros., 1949), pp. 97-99. Used by permission.
80	8	*The Evanston Assembly Report,* ed. W. A. Visser't Hooft (New York: Harper and Bros.), p. 113. Used by permission.
82	11	Acts 4:32
83	7	I Pet. 2:17
83	7	Eph. 2:19
83	7	Gal. 6:10
83	8	Phil. 3:20
84	1	I Cor. 15:21-22
87	3	*First Assembly of World Council of Churches,* p. 51.
87	18	*Ibid.,* p. 55
99	27	Rev. 5:12
102	11	Heb. 9
102	19	Heb. 12:2